The Laser Printer Handbook

Dow Jones-Irwin Desktop Publishing Library

Co-Authors

Larry Wood is the real author of this book. He designed the examples, created the figures, and wrote most of the text. He is also the person who spent many long hours at night making sure that the programs in the book worked correctly. It was only through his diligence and perserverance that the book was completed. Mr. Wood is an industry consultant, writer and technology expert who specalizes in finding innovative ways to use computers in business. One of his projects, for example, provided real-time computer information for a national news organization covering the 1988 presidential campaign

Mike Leube is the consulting technical author of this book. He, too, spent many hours making sure that all of the details are correct. In fact, much of the original impetus of the book is due to his understanding of laser printers and their business uses. Mr. Leube is a leading programmer who specializes in printing applications.

The Laser Printer Handbook

David Myers

DOW JONES-IRWIN
Homewood, Illinois 60430

This publication is designed to provide accurate and authoritative information in regard to the subject matter covered. It is sold with the understanding that the copyright holder is not engaged in rendering legal, accounting, or other professional service. If legal advice or other expert assistance is required, the services of a competent professional person should be sought.

Sponsoring editor: Susan Glinert Stevens, Ph.D.
Project editor: Karen Smith
Production manager: Carma Fazio
Cover design: Mark Swimmer
Design and typesetting: James Miller and ColorTech
Printer: Malloy Lithographing, Inc.

Library of Congress Cataloging-in-Publication Data

Myers, David.
   The laser printer handbook / David Myers.
      p.   cm.
   Includes index.
   ISBN 1-55623-133-4
   1. Printing, Practical—Laser use in.   2. Printers (Data processing systems)   I. Title.
   Z249.4.M93   1989
   686.2'314—dc19   89-1628
                                                                          CIP

Printed in the United States of America.

1 2 3 4 5 6 7 8 9 0 ML 6 5 4 3 2 1 0 9

Contents

Chapter 1

Introduction

Have you ever looked longingly at the advertisements for a laser printer and wondered how—just exactly how—to put graphics into your report? Or add a box for a picture on a page? Or get the laser printer to draw something as simple as a horizontal line to end each chapter in your new bestseller? You know the printer has the capabilities because you've seen the examples, but nowhere in the manual does it explain precisely what to do to get the output you want. That's what this book is all about.

This book consists of a set of practical, step-by-step examples that illustrate how to get your laser printer to do a number of different tasks. Of course, even these tasks are probably not *exactly* the ones you want for your work. For instance, you may want a horizontal line to be thicker, or in a different position than shown by the examples. And your business logo, and signature block (which you'll see how to print on stationery) are unique to you and your organization, so there's no way this book could describe the exact steps for creating those graphics. Therefore, along with the step-by-step instructions are extra illustrations and guides that show how to apply a particular example to your individual requirements.

Try the examples first. Then the supplementary information will make more sense and you'll see clearly how to get the print features you want. That way, you'll get the most out of your laser printer, and it will finally live up to your expectations.

Here are illustrations of the tasks covered in this book:

I go, and it is done: the bell invites me.
Hear it not, Duncan, for it is a knell
That summons thee to heaven, or to hell.

Scene 2

Lady Macbeth enters

LADY M. That which hath made them drunk hath made me bold;

Figure 4-17. Printed text illustrating bold and italic text fragments in a document.

ABC Computers
100 Megabyte Drive
Binary, CA 99999

Kyocera Unison, Inc.
3165 Adeline Street
Berkeley, California 94703

Figure 5-1. Printed business envelope with return and destination address.

Super-Co 1st Quarter Notables

* Revenue is up by 37%

* Net Profit has risen by 41%

* Employee count is up only 14%

Figure 6-3. Spruce up your presentation with borders (see Chapter 10 for examples).

	In CONGRESS, July 4, 1776.
1	
2	The unanimous Declaration of the
3	thirteen united States of America,
4	When in the course of human events it becomes
5	necessary for one people to dissolve the political
6	bands which have connected them with another, and
7	to assume among the powers of the earth, the
8	separate and equal station to which the Laws of

Figure 7-2. Declaration of Independence on a pleading document.

ORLANDO. I attend them with all respect and duty.

ROSALIND.(1) Young man, have you challenged Charles the wrestler?

ORLANDO. No, fair princess: he is the general challenger. I come but in, as others do, to try with him the strength of my youth.

———

1. Daughter of the banished Duke

Figure 8-2. Printed Horizontal Rule. If you want the rule and footnote at the bottom of the page, add returns prior to the sequence as necessary.

Beauty, truth and rarity,
Grace in all simplicity,
Here enclosed, in cinders lie.

Death is now the phoenix' nest;
And the turtle's loyal breast
To eternity doth rest.

Leaving no posterity,
'Twas not their infirmity,
It was married chastity.

Figure 9-2. Printed Vertical Rule; used to annotate or highlight selected paragraphs.

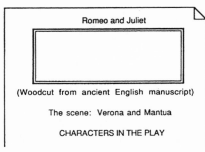

Romeo and Juliet

(Woodcut from ancient English manuscript)

The scene: Verona and Mantua

CHARACTERS IN THE PLAY

Figure 10-8. Printed box with double borders between paragraphs of text.

Three of the most likely candidates for the democratic nomination of President of the United States are Jesse Jackson, Gary Hart, and Michael Dukakis who is favored by many to beat Jesse Jackson in the final tally.

Figure 11-1. Scanners offer you the ability to mix graphic images with your text documents to convey messages much more effectively.

The downtown occupancy rate in our inner city has peaked dramatically in the past year, signalling a trend we must deal with.

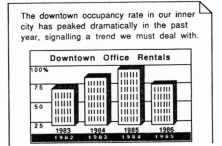

Figure 11-2. Business graphs can help tell a story much more effectively than just text alone.

Dear Stefanie,

Thank you for joining our expedition to Kathmandu next month. I will be sending you an itinerary within the week, so pack your duds!

Richard Bangs
Sobek Expeditions

Figure 11-4. Printed page with Logo used as letterhead.

Figure 12-1. Barcodes printed on Kyocera printer using Prescribe sequence on 3-up adhesive labels.

Figure 14-1. Many varieties of forms can be created with Prescribe sequences and stored on the IC card for use in your business.

By the way, although you don't need to know anything at all about the technology of laser printers to accomplish these examples, part of their descriptions include discussions of the pertinent printer features. Knowing about these features and the accompanying technology will help you apply the laser printer to specific tasks more effectively. There are, however, a few things you do need to know before starting.

WHAT YOU NEED TO KNOW

To use this book you need to know about:

- Your IBM® (or compatible) personal computer
- The program you're using to print
- Connecting and using your laser printer

The Computer You need to be familiar with your IBM (or compatible) personal computer. For the sake of brevity, this book refers to your computer as the PC or the Personal Computer whether it's an IBM, a Compaq® or one of the other MS-DOS® compatibles. You need to know how to run your PC and to use the more common DOS commands. In addition, you should understand how to create and save files, copy disks, and do other routine tasks.

The Program You also need to know about the particular program you're going to use for printing. For example, if you write letters with WordStar®, you need to know how to write the letters, save and load the necessary files, and print the letters using the WordStar commands. Although this book has specific instructions for some of the most popular word processing programs, you still need to know about your particular program.

The Printer Each printer has its own instructions for connecting the cables, loading the software for printing (called the printer drivers), and sending information from the computer to the printer. The printer manual shows how to attach the printer to the computer and the steps for loading the printer drivers. You also need to know about the routine jobs of loading paper, changing the toner cartridge, and so on.

WHAT THIS BOOK COVERS

Currently dozens of laser printers are on the market, and there are literally thousands of programs available ranging from word processing to spreadsheets to games. Many, if not most, of the programs will print on a laser printer. To cover all combinations of printers and programs would require volumes, not just a single book. So, to provide you with as much breadth as possible, this book covers several major word processing programs, other popular programs, and two popular laser printers.

The programs use for examples in this book are:

- MultiMate II®
- WordStar Professional®
- Microsoft WORD®
- Lotus 1-2-3®

The laser printers are:

- Hewlett-Packard LaserJet® Series II laser printer
- Kyocera F-1000A™ and the entire family of Kyocera laser printers

HOW TO USE THIS BOOK

Here are the steps for using the information in this book:

1. Review the table of contents. The table lists the various combinations of printer and program for each of the examples.

2. Find the combination of printer and program that you use, turn to the pages for the example, and read the step-by-step instructions.

This is primarily a book you can use to understand your laser printer, not how to use your software. If you don't use one of the programs in the examples, use the instructions for a similar program. For example, the WordStar program may be similar to your particular word processing program. In that case, read the examples for WordStar. You'll easily adjust to the examples, because most word processors have similar functions and features, and you can learn what you wanted to learn.

3 Try the example using your PC and laser printer.

4. Look at some of the supplementary comments to see how to apply the example to your particular situation.

5. Experiment with the example until you produce the printing exactly right for your tasks. Jot down the steps, including any printer sequences, to get the printing done. If any significant program sequences are involved, save them in their own files. You'll be able to re-use the sequences later without having to re-write them.

A WORD OF ENCOURAGEMENT

Printing graphic elements, and especially figuring out the sequences of commands for printing those elements, can be daunting. However, once you get the hang of it, using your laser is no more difficult than using DOS commands. Even more encouraging is that once you've written one sequence to print a specific graphic, that same sequence will work with other text in other files. Thus, you can build a repertoire of sequences that can be re-used as often as you need them. Eventually you'll be able to make your letters and reports look as goods as the advertisements that persuaded you to buy the laser printer in the first place.

Chapter 2

About Laser Printers

Laser printers are creating a printing revolution for PC users that rivals the earlier information revolution brought about by personal computers. Today, laser printing technology brings print quality and flexibility at a price and performance level unheard of even five years ago. It's often been said that the paperless office—once touted by manufacturers of personal computers—is mercifully obsolete, thanks to the invention of laser printers.

In this chapter, you'll learn a bit about the technology of laser printers and about the way you can get them to do your bidding. Two printers have been chosen for the examples in this book: the Hewlett-Packard LaserJet Series II and the Kyocera F-1000A.

The Hewlett-Packard LaserJet II is a popular laser printer supported by most programs today. The Kyocera is also a popular and powerful laser printer, with the ability to emulate seven different printers, including the HP LaserJet, and possesses an extensive graphics language as well. After reading this chapter, you'll have the background to make the examples in this book fit your needs.

THE KYOCERA F-1000A

The Kyocera F-1000A is a laser printer with a resolution of 300 dots per inch, both vertical and horizontal. It can print at a rate of 10 pages per minute, although some printing will be slower than the maximum rate, depending on the volume and complexity of each page. The printer has a paper cassette capacity of 250 pages.

One of the most valuable features of the Kyocera F-1000A printer is that it can emulate seven other popular printers on the market today:

- Teletype (TTY) or standard line printer
- IBM Graphics Printer®
- Diablo 630®
- Qume Sprint II®
- NEC Spinwriter®
- Epson FX-80®
- HP LaserJet Series II

This means that essentially the Kyocera is really seven printers in one. In other words, if you have software that works with any of those seven different printers, it will work just the same with the Kyocera. Just how do you make the Kyocera emulate one of these printers? By a simple choice available from the "driver" software that you use to run the printer. That choice lets you select the emulation mode for the appropriate driver.

PRINTER DRIVERS

Programs on your PC use "driver' software to communicate with peripheral devices, such as printers, connected to your PC. Driver software, as the name implies, is utility software that "drives," or controls a specific peripheral device. Because each device is engineered to perform in a certain way, driver software must be written for each particular device. Often, software companies will provide many different drivers for their products, so that you, as a customer, can choose the printer you want to use by simply installing the appropriate driver. Having multiple drivers in the software means that you can choose the driver for your particular printer.

Installing the driver involves the printer set-up routines in your program. Typically a one-time chore for each printer that you want to use, the set-up routine is normally a "set it and forget it" process. But now with the Kyocera's multiple emulation modes there's a twist—and this is where the value of emulation comes in handy. For instance, if you already have an old Qume printer, and purchase a new Kyocera, you don't need to change the driver in your software. Instead, you can just set the emulation mode in the printer to match the driver in your software. In other words, you make the printer match the software instead of making the software match the printer.

This unique feature gives you the best of both worlds because you get laser printing without having to modify your software. Considering that many older pieces of software don't even support laser printers, the emulation ability also relieves you of the unpleasant task of buying new software that will run with the laser printer. What's more, you can be sure that the laser printer will be able to print the files created with the older software, something not necessarily assured when you have to convert to a new program.

Look again at the list of printers the Kyocera can emulate, and you'll see that the HP LaserJet is included. Why? Because many programs only have a driver for one laser printer, and it is for the LaserJet. Therefore, you can use the Kyocera with those programs as well. In fact, the Kyocera's initial operating state (its default mode) is the LaserJet emulation. Thus, if your program supports the LaserJet, you simply install the Kyocera driver into your software and start to work. You don't have to switch emulation modes.

No matter what emulation mode you're using, you get an impressive text and graphics language for writing short programs to create the laser printing features so prominent on advertisements. The Kyocera language is called *Prescribe*.

The Prescribe Language

Prescribe is a high-level language built into every Kyocera laser printer. You can use Prescribe to embellish text and create simple graphics, such as placing boxes around paragraphs, changing fonts, or selecting new font sizes and typestyles. Essentially, Prescribe gives you printing capabilities not generally available with the printing commands in your word processing program.

Prescribe commands are simple messages that the Kyocera laser printer can interpret. Typically you embed Prescribe commands into the text in order to produce a special printing effect. When you print the file, the Prescribe commands are sent to the laser along with the text. The printer, however, recognizes that the commands are not actually text to be printed, but are instead commands to produce some sort of print feature, such as changing a font or drawing a line. A special start commands tell the laser printer where the Prescribe commands begin, and another special command indicates the end of the Prescribe commands.

The Kyocera examples in this book use a number of Prescribe commands. Working through the examples, you'll get a reasonably broad taste of the programming language and its capabilities. *The Kyocera Compact Laser Printer F-Series Programming Manual* is a recommended supplement to this book. You'll want it to experiment with the extended examples so you can apply them to your particular situations.

Prescribe Language Primer

Here's a brief primer to help familiarize yourself with the Prescribe Language basics. If you're unsure about Prescribe, read through this short section first before starting to work with the examples.

Prescribe commands are sometimes issued one at a time, but often are entered as a sequence of commands. However, two special commands are always used to signal the start and the end of a Prescribe sequence, even if the sequence consists of only one command. The command that signifies the *start* of a Prescribe sequence is: !R! (it must be a capital R). The command that signifies the *end* of the Prescribe sequence is EXIT;. (The semicolon after the word EXIT is part of the command, but is frequently inadvertently left out of programs as people are learning Prescribe. Results of forgetting the semicolon include blank pages, or pages without any text after the Prescribe sequence).

The purpose of these start and end commands is to identify Prescribe commands explicitly as a sequence, even when the sequence is embedded in the middle of text. While receiving the text for printing, the printer continually searches for the !R! command. Whenever the three-character sequence "!R!" appears, the printer recognizes it and knows that the text immediately following consists of one or more Prescribe commands. Those commands are to be interpreted and acted upon, not printed. The printer executes each of the commands in turn, until it finds an EXIT command. The printer then knows the sequence is done and the text following the EXIT command is simply to be printed, not interpreted.

Prescribe commands are short, simple words or acronyms. The acronyms represent a description of what the command controls. For instance, one Prescribe command is SPD, which stands for Set Pen Diameter, and controls the thickness of a line that you want drawn. As an aid to learning the commands in this book, the letters (or word) that form the acronyms are capitalized in the explanation of each example.

Here's an example that shows the nature of the commands and the "embedded" sequence concept. Notice in the illustration that the Prescribe start and end commands are embedded in the middle of the poem. This is what the text and embedded sequence will look like on your PC screen before printing. This particular sequence is for drawing a horizontal ruled line .05" wide (because the pen diameter is set with the SPD command to .05). If the rest of the Prescribe sequence looks indecipherable, don't worry. It will all become clear and easy to use after you've studied a few of the examples later in this book.

```
Even as the sun with purple-coloured face
Had ta'en his last leave of the weeping morn,
Rose-cheeked Adonis hied him to the chase;
Hunting he loved, but love he laughed to scorn.
    Sick-thoughted Venus makes amain unto him,
    And like a bold-faced suitor 'gins to woo him.

!R!UNIT I;SPD .05;DRP 2,0;EXIT;

'Thrice fairer than myself,' thus she began,
'The field's chief flower, sweet above compare,
Stain to all nymphs, more lovely than a man,
More white and red than doves or roses are;
    Nature that made thee with herself at strife
    Saith that the world hath ending with thy life.
```

Figure 2-1. Prescribe Sequence for Horizontal Rule. Notice the space before and after the sequence, and the corresponding space in the printed text.

The next illustration shows what the poem looks like after it has been printed on the Kyocera. Note that the Prescribe sequence has been removed, and in its place is a horizontal rule.

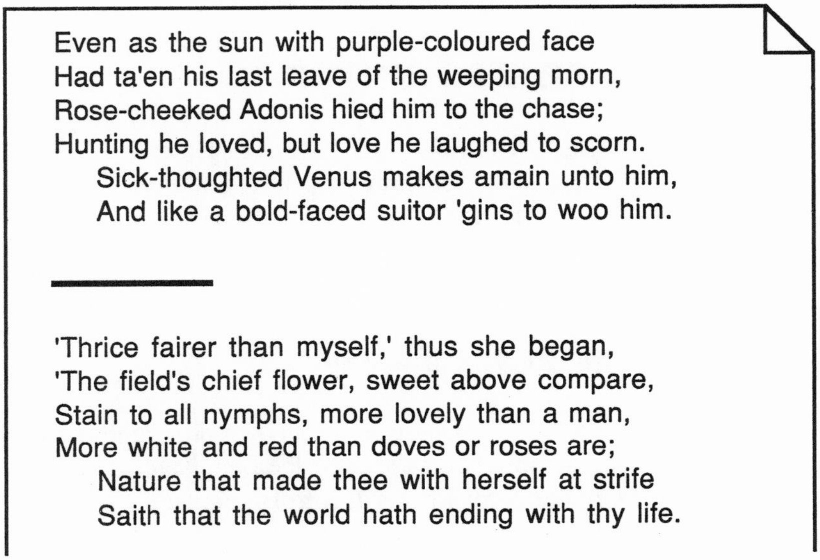

Even as the sun with purple-coloured face
Had ta'en his last leave of the weeping morn,
Rose-cheeked Adonis hied him to the chase;
Hunting he loved, but love he laughed to scorn.
Sick-thoughted Venus makes amain unto him,
And like a bold-faced suitor 'gins to woo him.

'Thrice fairer than myself,' thus she began,
'The field's chief flower, sweet above compare,
Stain to all nymphs, more lovely than a man,
More white and red than doves or roses are;
Nature that made thee with herself at strife
Saith that the world hath ending with thy life.

Figure 2-2. Printed Horizontal Rule.

THE HP LASERJET PRINTER

The Hewlett-Packard LaserJet printer is also a 300 dot-per-inch laser printer, with a maximum printing rate of 8 pages per minute. Like the Kyocera, printing will not usually occur at the maximum rate. The actual page printing rate will depend on the quantity and complexity of information on each page.

The PCL Language

The HP LaserJet also has its own programming language, similar in some respects to Kyocera's Prescribe Language. The LaserJet language is called PCL, short for Printer Control Language. Unlike the Kyocera's Prescribe "English-like" language, however, the LaserJet language is composed of rather cryptic escape sequences.

PCL Primer

An escape sequence is a computer term for a sequence of one or more characters used to control a peripheral device such as a printer or modem. Escape sequences are often embedded in text to be printed or to be transmitted over telephone lines. An escape sequence must begin with some special character (much in the same way as the !R! start command in Prescribe) so the device receiving the text can identify where the sequence begins.

In the case of PCL, that special character is called the escape character. Because it's used by many programs, the escape character often has its own key on the keyboard, usually labelled Esc. What does the escape character actually look like? Unfortunately, you can't see it because it's a non-printable character. In the text in this book, it is shown as E_C (shorthand for Escape Character), but you never see that on the screen.

Even though you can't see the escape character, a printer or modem can and then knows that the sequence of characters immediately following are not to be printed or transmitted, but are instead to be interpreted as commands. The HP Laserjet's PCL language uses escape sequences in the same way a Kyocera printer uses Prescribe to control the printer, to change fonts, print certain graphic images, and so on.

Using the Esc key as the character to start a sequence may pose a problem because word processing programs also use the escape character for some of their functions. Thus, pressing the Esc key causes the program to do something instead of just indicating the start of the printer escape sequence. Each word processing program deals with this difficulty in its own way, which means you may have to slightly alter the way you use the program.

Conceptually, the Prescribe commands and the PCL escape sequences are, in fact, the same because both languages have the same goal: to be able to control a laser printer from software running on the PC. One difference between PCL and Prescribe is that the PCL escape sequences are character-based while Prescribe command sequences are word-based, which makes Prescribe easier for you to understand. Another difference is that PCL has no universal stop command equivalent to the Prescribe EXIT. Instead, each command has its own specific character to indicate the end of the sequence. Of course, another difference is that each language has its own features and capabilities, as you'll see later on in this book.

To illustrate the use of PCL, here's the same example used in the Prescribe Primer section for drawing a horizontal line, except this time using PCL to draw the line.

```
Even as the sun with purple-coloured face
Had ta'en his last leave of the weeping morn,
Rose-cheeked Adonis hied him to the chase;
Hunting he loved, but love he laughed to scorn.
    Sick-thoughted Venus makes amain unto him,
    And like a bold-faced suitor 'gins to woo him.
<-*c600A<-*c15B<-*c0P

'Thrice fairer than myself,' thus she began,
'The field's chief flower, sweet above compare,
Stain to all nymphs, more lovely than a man,
More white and red than doves or roses are;
    Nature that made thee with herself at strife
    Saith that the world hath ending with thy life.
```

Figure 2-3. PCL Sequence for Horizontal Rule. Notice the space only after the sequence. The corresponding space printed will be text.

If it seems confusing to you now, that's to be expected. After you've tried a few of these PCL sequences yourself, the mystery will vanish; by the time you've completed most of the examples, you'll have mastered PCL and can put it to good use.

Even as the sun with purple-coloured face
Had ta'en his last leave of the weeping morn,
Rose-cheeked Adonis hied him to the chase;
Hunting he loved, but love he laughed to scorn.
  Sick-thoughted Venus makes amain unto him,
  And like a bold-faced suitor 'gins to woo him.

'Thrice fairer than myself,' thus she began,
'The field's chief flower, sweet above compare,
Stain to all nymphs, more lovely than a man,
More white and red than doves or roses are;
  Nature that made thee with herself at strife
  Saith that the world hath ending with thy life.

Figure 2-4. Printed Horizontal Rule.

By comparing the output from the two printers, and you'll find they look the same, even though the commands are from two different languages, and the poem was printed on two different printers.

One final note: like the Prescribe manual, the *LaserJet Series II Printer Technical Reference Manual* is also a recommended supplement for this book.

Chapter 3

Using Word Processing Software with Your Laser Printer

This chapter serves as a preface to the examples in this book. Each piece of software, including the software for the laser printers, has its own quirks and idiosyncrasies. For instance, the process to enter an escape sequence in Microsoft WORD is a specific set of keystrokes not applicable to any other program. Rather than constantly reminding you about the unusual aspects of each piece of the software in the rest of the book, they're consolidated here.

This chapter also tells you about other common issues involved with laser printing, such as how to overcome pagination problems when the processing between the printer and the program conflict.

Read this chapter before trying the examples described in the later chapters. You'll save a lot of time and frustration. And if you seem to be having insurmountable problems with your printer, skim through this chapter again and you may find the answers.

WHAT IF THE DOCUMENT IS MORE THAN ONE PAGE?

More often than not, you'll be working with a multiple-page document, and that may cause a problem with pagination. The typical symptom of the problem is blank pages.

The reason for the problem is that word processing programs treat embedded laser printer commands as ordinary text and counts it as part of the text for figuring out the pagination. However, the printer does not print those commands; instead the printer reads them, interprets their instructions, *removes them from the printing*, and then draws a graphic or performs some other function. Consequently, the process of removing the commands from the printed text throws off the word processing program's page count which can leave a "hole" in the text.

The most common problem is that commands embedded on separate lines in the text are counted as actual lines for printing. This causes the word processing program to count the carriage returns after each command as new lines of text. For multiple page documents, the extra line count often causes the word processor to force page breaks in the middle of the pages following your commands. If you encounter this problem, here are some solutions.

Enter Commands on One Line

One solution is to enter the commands together on one line, without carriage returns. Most of the examples in this book show one command per line. Seeing the commands on separate lines is not only easier to read, it's easier to understand the sequence of commands and what they do. However, both

Prescribe and PCL allow commands to be typed continuously on a line without entering a carriage return after each individual command. This simple solution will help reduce the problem of incorrect pagination.

For example, if you enter a sequence of commands that takes two lines of space, you can reduce that page's length by two lines to accommodate the sequence. The pagination will then come out correctly.

Use "Include" Features for Flexibility

Another method of solving the pagination problem (and creating more flexibility for your programming sequences in the process) is to use a feature known in many word processing programs as the "include" feature. It lets you use a separate file as a part of the word processing file you're working with. That is, you can include one file in another one. By putting the programming sequence for the laser printer in the include file, the printer will see the file, but the word processing program won't use it as part of its page count. Most word processors have this feature, but it is called something different in each one, and has its own implementation style.

The include feature in Microsoft WORD

Microsoft has implemented its include feature in WORD specifically so you can include separate files that contain laser printer command sequences without affecting pagination. To take advantage of the include feature, you create a separate document that contains only the laser printer commands that you want to include in your text document. In general, here are the steps to follow:

1. Create a new, unnamed document.

2. Enter the desired laser printer commands in the new document. In this document, you can use carriage returns after each command for readability and ease of editing because they won't be counted by WORD during pagination.

3. After entering the laser printer sequence, test it by printing directly to the laser printer. If the sequence is successful and the laser printer prints what you expected, save the document with an appropriate name such as BOX3x5.DOC (which would be a descriptive file name for the sequence to draw a box 3 inches by 5 inches). When you save the document as a file, select the Unformatted option, because WORD cannot include a file saved as a formatted file.

Now, whenever you want a 3" x 5" box in the text, you can "include" the file by entering WORD's appropriate .P. code in your text at the position where the box is to occur. WORD won't count the programming sequence as lines of text, but the printer will read the sequence, interpret the commands, and draw the box.

Using the example of the 3" x 5" box file, the .P. code to enter in your text would be .P. B:\BOX3x5.DOC, 3. The B: assumes that the file is stored on a disk in the B drive, and the 3 at the end of the command is a WORD parameter telling the printer to allow 3 inches of space for the box.

After entering the command, select it, choose Character from WORD's Format menu, and then choose Hidden Text. Making the text hidden means that WORD will not count the .P. command as text to be printed either.

When you print the text file, WORD includes the BOX3x5.DOC file at the position of the .P. command, and sends both files to the printer. The text gets printed, the box gets drawn, and the pagination stays correct.

Another benefit of using include files is that you can create and save a variety of programming sequences, and then include them into other text files. Thus, you don't have to re-type the sequence each time you want to use it; you can simply call the sequence with the .P. command. If you use this process, you'll eventually create a library of include files for all of the different type of special laser printing that you want to accomplish.

The include feature in MultiMate

MultiMate does not currently have the include feature as part of its word processing commands. If later releases add the feature, it will probably work much in the same fashion as the WORD feature.

The include feature in WordStar

WordStar's feature for including separate documents is referred to as nesting or chaining files. Just as in WORD, you can create sequences of Prescribe or PCL commands, store the sequences in a separate document, and "chain" or add them on to the text file during printing. The chained file won't alter pagination.

In general, here are the steps to follow to use a chained file:

1. Clear the screen and create a new, unnamed document.

2. Enter the desired laser printer commands in the new document. You can add carriage returns after each laser printer command for readability and ease of editing. The carriage returns won't be counted by WordStar during pagination.

3. Test the sequence by printing directly to the printer. If the sequence works as you want it, store it with an appropriate name such as MapUS.PKG

(for instance, this sequence might be for a graphic of the map of the United States).

Now, whenever you want the map in your text, you can chain the file by using MultiMate's .FI command. An example of the command is:

.FI b:MapUS.pkg.

Put the .FI command where you want the map to occur in the text. When you print your document WordStar will pull in this "chained" file, and send it to the printer. The printer will read the file and draw the map. The pagination will not be affected.

ENTERING ESCAPE CHARACTERS IN PROGRAMS

The HP PCL language uses an escape character to begin each PCL command. In this book, the escape character is noted as E_C, and it has the ASCII code 27. *You **do not** enter the PCL escape character by pressing the Esc key on your keyboard. Instead, you must enter a sequence of keystrokes that the word processing program understands as ASCII 27.*

Escape Characters in Microsoft WORD

To enter an escape character in WORD, you must hold down the Alt key while typing the characters 2 and 7 from the numeric keypad. The 2 and 7 will not show up on the screen, but a left arrow appears to indicate the location of the escape character.

Escape Characters in MultiMate

To enter an escape character in MultiMate you must hold down the Alt key and the A key while typing the characters 2 and 7 from the numeric keypad. The sequence appears on the screen as μ27.

Escape Characters in WordStar

To enter the escape character in WordStar, press Control-P and then escape key. The character will appear on the screen as ^[.

Escape Characters in Lotus 1-2-3

In the Set-up string, you can enter the escape character by entering \027. However, this character string will not work in the work area. In the work area, you must enter |\027. (The | is the uppercase backslash.)

PCL PROGRAM ISSUES

PCL, when compared to Prescribe, tends to be cryptic and arcane. It was written to be a compact, powerful printer control language primarily for professional programmers who might want to embed printer commands as features in their commercial programs. As an end user, you were never supposed to see the PCL commands.

However, because many programs offer only limited printer functions, you're faced with a dilemma: accept the limitations, or learn PCL. The examples in this book show you how to use some of the common PCL features, without requiring that you become a PCL expert.

Because PCL commands begin with an escape character, they are often referred to as escape sequences. The term escape sequence and command are used interchangeably in this book.

You'll notice that many of the PCL examples in this book have individual commands on separate lines. This layout improves readability, and helps you to see what the commands are for, but they can be compressed as a continuous stream of typing if necessary.

You can also shorten the PCL sequences by combining commands. When reviewing two or more commands for combining, if the parameterized character and the group character (always the first two characters after the escape character itself) are identical, then you can combine them. When combining two or more commands, each alphabetic character must be lowercase except the last, which must be uppercase. To see how combining works, review the example in Chapter 7, which uses combined commands extensively.

Resetting the HP LaserJet

Sometimes changing the default settings on the LaserJet can result in some confusing printing instructions. If you need to reset the defaults in order to try a new sequence of commands, just send the PCL command E_CE to reset the printer's options back to the original default settings.

Using PCL from BASIC

You can use PCL with BASIC, but if you do, be forewarned: you have to know and understand the nature of BASIC as well as PCL in order to use the two languages together. Nevertheless, using them together provides much more flexibility than word processing program options. By using BASIC (or any other programming language, for that matter), you can do some marvelous things with PCL.

If at First You Don't Succeed ... With PCL

If you're having difficulty with the printer, follow these steps to do some troubleshooting.

PCL Command Errors

Read through your code, and make sure the command mnemonics are all spelled correctly. The mnemonic is the short acronym that identifies the command. Also make sure that the escape character is in place and the parameters are correct. If you're working with combined commands, check that the first two characters are identical and can be dropped and that all alphabetic characters are lowercase, except the last character. The last character indicates to the printer the end of the command sequence.

PRESCRIBE LANGUAGE ISSUES

To improve readability, the examples in this book show Prescribe commands in uppercase, with a space between the command mnemonic and its parameters. Neither the uppercasing nor the space is required. If you prefer, all the typing can be lowercase and compressed without spaces.

In fact, in Lotus 1-2-3 you should eliminate the spaces, because you'll need all the characters you can get in the Setup string, which is only 39 characters long.

Notes About Various Prescribe Commands

The UNIT command, which specifies the units of measurement by the printer, will not appear in all of the examples. The default UNIT parameter is

I, for Inches. Because most of the measurements are in inches, adding the UNIT command is unnecessary in most of the Prescribe sequences.

To return the Kyocera's defaults to their original settings, send the Prescribe command RES to the printer. The complete sequence to send is: !R!RES;EXIT;. Usually you'll want to reset the defaults after each sequence so the next one can start again from scratch. You'll also want to reset when a test sequence produces some unexpected printing results.

You can determine the Kyocera's settings by using the command STAT (for status). This will cause the status page to print so you can review all of your settings. The simplest sequence to get a status report is: "!R!STAT;EXIT;".

In most Prescribe examples, the EXIT command has no parameters. However, on some occasions you may not want the carriage return following the EXIT command to be taken literally. By adding the E parameter — "EXIT,E;" — you can tell Prescribe to ignore the next carriage return.

Unwanted Pages

Sometimes you'll get extra blank pages even in the simplest of Prescribe sequences. If you're using the RES command at the end of a sequence, try removing it. Another cause of blank pages sometimes is the page numbering feature in the word processing software. Turn that feature off from the program to see if that solves the problem.

Using Prescribe from BASIC

As with the HP PCL language, you can use Prescribe with other programming languages, such as BASIC. Being able to combine two programming languages offers much more flexibility than the options available from a single word processing program, but you do have to understand both languages to make the commands work properly. Nevertheless, if you are able to use languages together, you can make your Kyocera printer print wonderful images.

If at First You Don't Succeed ... With Prescribe

If you're having difficulty with the printer, first get a status page. Make sure that the printer options are set the way you expect them.

Incorrect Emulation Mode

If you're sending an HP sequence to the Kyocera, and emulation is set for another printer (the Epson, for example), the sequence won't work. Check the P1 option on the status page, and set the printer properly. This can be done directly on the control panel with some models, and it can always be done with the FRPO command or the SEM command.

Prescribe Command Errors

Each sequence must start with the string !R!. Read through your code, and make sure the mnemonics are all spelled correctly. The mnemonic is the acronym that stands for a particular command, such as MRP for Move Relative Position. Check that the parameters are correct and separated with commas or single quotes. Make sure a semicolon follows each command, and finally, don't forget the EXIT command, which also must be followed by a semicolon.

Chapter 4

Selecting Font Styles and Sizes for Your Text

Before the age of laser printers, secretaries did most of the word processing, using typewriters and later, daisy-wheel printers. There were usually only a few type styles available — most notably, Pica and Elite.

All of that changed with the advent of laser printers. Now that the sophistication and power of laser printers have brought many typesetting options and terms out of the print shop and into the office, you'll benefit by knowing some of the more common terms. This chapter covers the sometimes-confusing world of fonts, and the process of selecting them for your printing.

Because the word processing programs chosen for the examples in this book all deal effectively with selecting fonts, this chapter departs from the format of discussing each specific printer/word processor combination. Instead, the examples in this chapter focus on the use of printer languages for font selection. The selection processes apply to word processors in general.

WHAT IS A FONT?

Traditionally, printers and publishers define a font as a complete set of type in one typeface, size, style, and other characteristics. If you italicize the text, or boldface it, you are—according to the more traditional definition—changing the font.

However, because of the way computers and laser printers deal with printable characters, the computer industry often refers to fonts and their characteristics in a slightly different manner. Underlining, boldfacing, and italics are often considered *features* of a particular font, not a separate font. Although this distinction is a small difference in definition, the use of the term "font" can nevertheless be confusing, especially if both definitions are used interchangeably.

Typeface

The distinguishing element of a font is the typeface, which refers to the design or artistic appearance of the characters.

Figure 4-1. Different typefaces are created by artists who design characters for different uses, moods and effects.

Size

The size of a font is the vertical measure of the character from the baseline to the top of the characters (not including descenders). Size is usually stated in printer's points, or points for short. Traditionally, a point is 72 and 27/100ths of an inch, but is calculated at 1/72 of an inch in the computer world. Common font sizes are 10 point or 12 point type. To illustrate the difference in sizes: here is 9 point, 10 point, 12 point, 14 point, and 18 point.

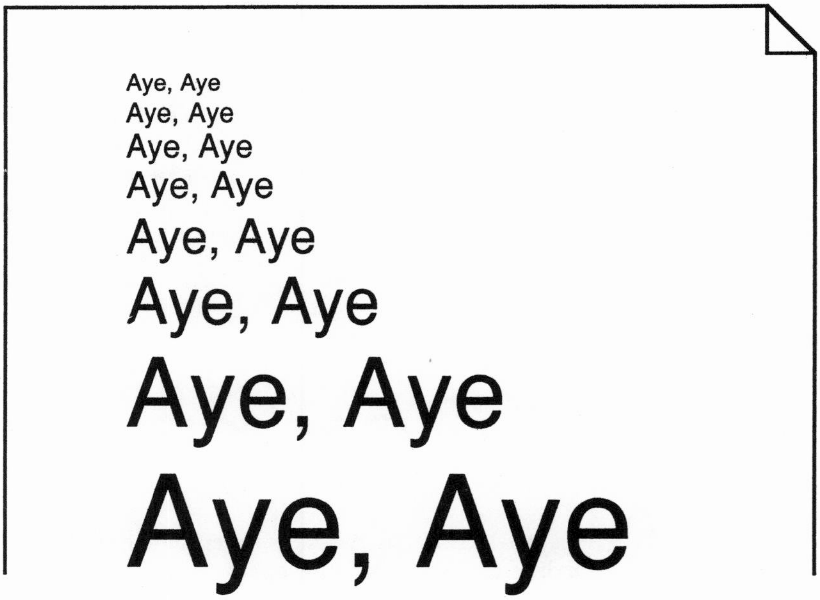

Figure 4-2. A variety of point sizes are available on most laser printers.

Pitch

There are two types of pitch, (sometimes referred to as spacing) that affect fonts. Typewriters normally only allow fixed pitch characters. That is, each character takes up the same amount of horizontal space on the line. For example, 10 pitch means there are 10 characters per inch.

Figure 4-3. As you can see, fixed spacing creates irregular interletter spacing, because it gives characters of different width equal — fixed — space.

Typewriters have a fixed pitch because they are mechanical devices, and a fixed pitch simplifies the mechanics of the horizontal movement of the print head. Typesetting machines, however, use a film process that is not limited to fixed pitch, and therefore use the fonts that are proportionally spaced.

Proportionally spaced fonts are designed so that a narrow character takes up less horizontal space than a wide character, and each character has its own specific width. The space between each character, called the interletter space, remains the same. Because of this design, proportionally spaced fonts do not specify a pitch.

While a proportional font creates its own peculiar complexities, the printed page takes on a beauty and readability far better than with simpler fixed pitch fonts. Another major benefit of proportionally-spaced fonts is that more text can be placed on a page, without the page seeming to be "packed" with text.

Figure 4-4. Proportional fonts have equal interletter spacing.

Stroke Weight

Stroke weight (or simply weight) is the width or thickness of each stroke on a character. Usually, the standard offered in laser printers is the common, or medium weight. Heavier stroke weights produce boldfaced characters, which are also almost always available in the same typeface on laser printers. At the other end of the stroke weight spectrum are "light" typefaces. The opposite of boldfacing, light typefaces deemphasize words. The option for light typefaces is not as common on laser printers as boldfacing.

William Shakespeare

William Shakespeare

Figure 4-5. Medium weight fonts are the most common. The bold font below is slightly heavier, and also has wider spacing to accomodate the slightly thicker strokes of each character.

Shear

The shear of a font refers to the slant of the characters. There are two common shears: italic and upright. Italicizing a font slants each character to the right. An upright font has no slant. Upright characters are oriented at a 90 degree angle relative to the lines on a page. Upright fonts are sometimes called Roman fonts, although the term Roman is also used to refer to the familiar Times Roman typeface. Another shear option is reverse italic, which—like the light weight—is relatively uncommon and is not usually offered in laser printers.

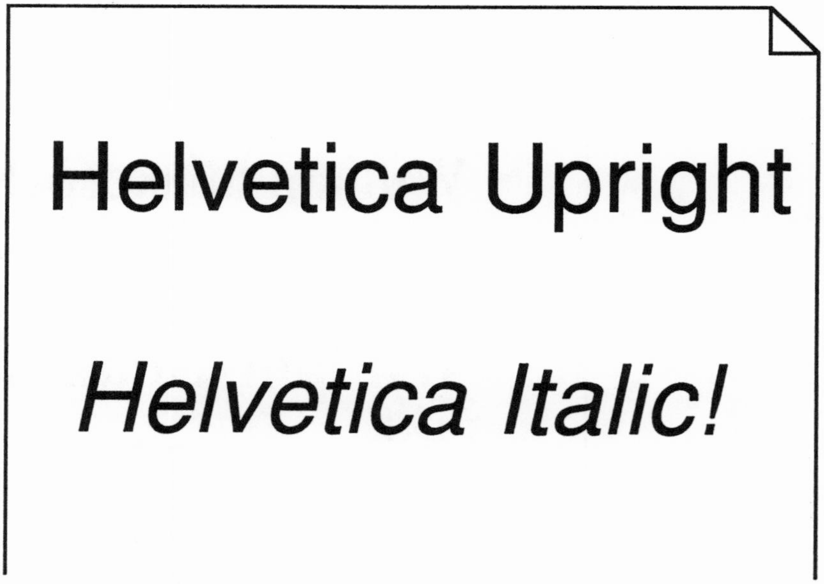

Helvetica Upright

Helvetica Italic!

Figure 4-6. Altering the shear of a font can have a striking effect on the visual image portrayed on the printed page.

Orientation

The orientation of the fonts when the characters are printed can be either *portrait* or *landscape*. Portrait refers to the more common orientation of text on a page, running across the narrow width of the paper, as in this book, or on a business letter. The term comes from the common orientation of portraits of people, which are almost always painted in a vertical or upright format.

Landscape orientation is printed the long way on the page (sideways), as in overhead transparencies, children's books, or instructional manuals that contain lots of graphics. The term landscape brings to mind landscape paintings, most often painted in a horizontal format.

Strictly speaking, orientation is not an attribute traditionally associated with the fonts themselves. Rather, it is a page layout term. When laying out a page, printers would simply orient the page in a landscape or portrait fashion by turning the paper. Since laser printers can't turn the paper, they turn or "rotate" the fonts instead. Thus, orientation has come to be associated with the fonts in laser printers.

Figure 4-7. Portrait orientation, on the left, is placed along the width of the page, while landscape orientation is placed along the length, as shown on the right.

Another term you may encounter is *leading* (pronounced "ledding"). Leading is another term not actually part of a font's characteristics, but refers to the white space between each row of text. Leading, like size, is measured in points, and is available as an option is some word processors. The term originates from the old typesetting days when printers put hot strips of lead metal between rows of text to achieve the proper line spacing. Like most other typesetting terms, this one stuck even though today leading is done on word processors electronically instead of by hand with metal.

SELECTING FONTS WITH ALL THE TRIMMINGS

In the following examples, you'll see how to use Prescribe and PCL commands to select typefaces, styles and sizes for the fonts you want to use in your documents. Using the commands typically provides more flexibility and choice of fonts than options in your word processing program.

Before You Print

In many cases, using the printer drivers specifically named for the Kyocera or HP LaserJet will interfere with some of the font and typestyle changes. The safest bet is to use the DRAFT, TTY or PLAIN style drivers that are available. The reason that using one of these three drivers works well is because all three assume the printer has none of its own processing capability. In other words, the drivers assume your printer has the same capabilities as a standard teletype machine—print fixed-pitch, single-sized characters, perform carriage returns, and ring a bell. That assumed simplicity, in turn, means that your word processing program will send almost anything you type to the printer untampered, which, because you're typing commands that should not get processed, is exactly what you want. So, if you encounter difficulties with the font changes, experiment with different drivers until you find one that will allow you to send commands directly to the printer with no intermediate processing by the word processing program.

USING FONTS IN THE KYOCERA LASER PRINTER

Some word processors are oblivious to Prescribe commands, and you can place them anywhere in the text without fear of retribution. Almost always though, the ending of a line containing Prescribe commands will be affected, so placing Prescribe commands at the beginning or somewhere in the middle of a line is only reasonable if your lines are shorter than the maximum allowed, and you have made specific adjustments to compensate for the spaces taken up by the Prescribe sequence.

In most cases, and for most word processors (usually the more sophisticated ones), Prescribe commands need to be hidden. That is, they need to be placed in inconspicuous places in the text where their presence will not affect word spacing or line endings when the printer processes and then removes the commands from the text.

Usually this means placing them at the end of the last line of a paragraph. Alternatively, the commands can be placed in the blank line between paragraphs.

Italicizing a Paragraph of Text

Use the following sequence of Prescribe commands to italicize text. Place the sequence at the end of the last line in the paragraph preceding the text to be italicized. If there isn't enough room on the last line, place the commands on a blank line between the paragraphs.

Command	Explanation
!R!	staRt Prescribe sequence
FONT 55;	Select Helvetica italic 8 point FONT*
EXIT;	EXIT Prescribe sequence

The FONT command changes all of the text following the sequence to the newly selected font. Therefore, to return to the previous font (or turn off the italicizing), you enter a similar sequence which calls the original font back.

Command	Explanation
!R!	staRt Prescribe sequence
FONT 13;	Select Helvetica roman 8 point FONT *
EXIT;	EXIT Prescribe sequence

* See the Resident Fonts Table in the Programming Manual

```
Let the bird of loudest lay,
On the sole Arabian tree,
Herald sad and trumpet be,
To whose sound chaste wings obey.
!R!FONT 55;EXIT;
But thou shrieking harbinger,
Foul precurrer of the fiend,
Augur of the fever's end,
To this troop come thou not near!
!R!FONT 13;EXIT;
From this session interdict
Every fowl of tyrant wing,
Save the eagle, feath'red king:
Keep the obsequy so strict.
```

Figure 4-8. Prescribe Sequence italicizing a paragraph of text, and returning to the upright style.

By using this technique of inserting Prescribe sequences between paragraphs, you can easily control the shear, as well as the weight and the typeface of a font.

Let the bird of loudest lay,
On the sole Arabian tree,
Herald sad and trumpet be,
To whose sound chaste wings obey.

But thou shrieking harbinger,
Foul precurrer of the fiend,
Augur of the fever's end,
To this troop come thou not near!

From this session interdict
Every fowl of tyrant wing,
Save the eagle, feath'red king:
Keep the obsequy so strict.

Figure 4-9. Printed paragraphs, with both upright and italic styles.

Boldfacing and Italicizing Subheads

Subheads often serve to guide the reader to just the right area of a manual or book, or to increase readability by setting text fragments in different styles. In this example, you'll see how to boldface and italicize text fragments and subheads.

Command	Explanation
!R!	staRt Prescribe sequence
FONT 4;	Select Times Roman Bold 10 point FONT *
EXIT;	EXIT Prescribe sequence

This FONT command will boldface all of the text following the sequence. By changing the FONT command, you can then change the next text to italic.

Command	Explanation
!R!	staRt Prescribe sequence
FONT 3;	Select Times Roman italic 10 point FONT *
EXIT;	EXIT Prescribe sequence

This FONT command will change all of the text following it to italic. To return the text to normal, roman type, change the FONT command again.

Command	Explanation
!R!	staRt Prescribe sequence
FONT 2;	Select Times Roman 10 point FONT *
EXIT;	EXIT Prescribe sequence

* See the Resident Fonts Table in the Programming Manual

```
I go, and it is done: the bell invites me.
Hear it not, Duncan, for it is a knell
That summons thee to heaven, or to hell.
!R!FONT 4;EXIT;


                   Scene 2!R!FONT 3;EXIT;

Lady Macbeth enters
!R!FONT 2;EXIT;
LADY M. That which hath made them drunk hath
made me bold;
```

Figure 4-10. Prescribe Sequence for bolding and italicizing subheads and fragments in text. Note that the sequence can be after the text fragment, or between paragraphs.

I go, and it is done: the bell invites me.
Hear it not, Duncan, for it is a knell
That summons thee to heaven, or to hell.

Scene 2

Lady Macbeth enters

LADY M. That which hath made them drunk hath made me bold;

Figure 4-11. Printed text illustrating bold and italic text fragments in a document.

Dealing Effectively with Larger Fonts

When it comes to printing text in a larger font, the main problem is matching the font size with the number of lines per inch to be printed on a page. The bigger the font, the less number of lines per inch. Most word processing programs default to common line settings, usually either 6 or 8 lines per inch. This setting accommodates 8 to 12 point type nicely, but is too many lines for larger type sizes. If you don't re-set the number of lines per inch you'll often run out of leading between the lines.

This next example shows how to increase the leading with a Prescribe command. You'll see how to select a large size typeface for the title of a document, and adjust the leading to accommodate it.

Command	Explanation
!R!	staRt Prescribe sequence
FONT 10;	Select Helvetica Bold 14.4 point FONT*
UNIT P;	Set the UNIT of measure to Printer's points
SLS 17;	Set Line Spacing to 17 points
EXIT;	EXIT Prescribe sequence

* See the Resident Fonts Table in the Programming Manual

The FONT command will change all of the text following the sequence to the newly selected font. To make line spacing easier, set the UNIT command so it's in Printer's points, and then set the spacing to about 20% greater than the point size selected for the larger font. The 20% allows for easy reading of the text.

```
!R!FONT 10;UNIT P;SLS 17;EXIT;
              The Complete Works

                     of

              William Shakespeare
```

Figure 4-12. Prescribe Sequence used to print larger type sizes, necessitating the adjustment of the leading, or line size.

The Complete Works

of

William Shakespeare

Figure 4-13. Printed text in large type.

USING FONTS IN THE HP LASERJET

Although many word processing programs are oblivious to PCL commands, and you can place them anywhere in the text, a better practice is to hide the commands. Unhidden commands affect the text by extending the lines the commands are on. If you do want to place the commands in the text, or your program doesn't have a text hiding capability, only place PCL commands at the beginning or middle of a line if it has sufficient space to accommodate the commands, and you have made specific adjustments to account for the spaces taken up by the PCL sequence.

To hide commands, you usually have two options. First, you can place them in some inconspicuous place in the text, typically at the end of a paragraph, and not in the middle of a line. Putting the commands on a separate line between paragraphs is another inconspicuous location. Second, some programs have a specific command (usually labeled Hide) just for the purpose of putting commands that the program ignores in the text. Printer commands are the most common form of hidden commands, although outlining options and formatting features may also be hidden.

The following examples show typical sequences of commands that should be hidden in the text. Note that some the PCL sequences are condensed for ease of typing. Refer to Chapter 3 for instructions on condensing PCL commands.

Italicizing a Paragraph of Text

The following sequence italicizes all the text that comes after the sequence, until you enter another sequence to return the text to its previous font (or some other font). Enter this PCL sequence at the either end of the last line of the paragraph preceding the text to be italicized or, if there isn't enough room, on a blank line between the paragraphs.

Command	Explanation
E_C&l0O	Select Landscape Orientation
E_C(8U	select Roman 8 symbol set
E_C(s1p8v1s3b4T	Select Helvetica italic 8 point FONT*

The FONT command will change all of the text following the sequence to the newly selected italic font. The next sequence "turns off" italics and returns the text to its original typeface.

Command	Explanation
E_C&l0O	Select Landscape Orientation*
E_C(8U	select Roman 8 symbol set
E_C(s1p8v0s0b4T	Select Helvetica roman 8 point FONT *

* See the Resident Fonts Table in the Programming Manual

```
Let the bird of loudest lay,
On the sole Arabian tree,
Herald sad and trumpet be,
To whose sound chaste wings obey.
<-&l0O<-(8U<-(s1p8v1s3b4T
But thou shrieking harbinger,
Foul precurrer of the fiend,
Augur of the fever's end,
To this troop come thou not near!
<-&l0O<-(8U<-(s1p8v0s0b4T
From this session interdict
Every fowl of tyrant wing,
Save the eagle, feath'red king:
Keep the obsequy so strict.
```

Figure 4-14. PCL Sequence italicizing a paragraph of text, and returning to the upright style.

Let the bird of loudest lay,
On the sole Arabian tree,
Herald sad and trumpet be,
To whose sound chaste wings obey.

But thou shrieking harbinger,
Foul precurrer of the fiend,
Augur of the fever's end,
To this troop come thou not near!

From this session interdict
Every fowl of tyrant wing,
Save the eagle, feath'red king:
Keep the obsequy so strict.

Figure 4-15. Printed paragraphs, with both upright and italic styles.

Boldfacing and Italicizing Subheads

Putting subheads into different typestyles helps guide the reader to sections of a manual or book and, at the same time, increases readability. In this example, you'll learn how to boldface and italicize text fragments and subheads in your documents.

Command	Explanation
E_C&l0O	Select Landscape Orientation*
E_C(8	select Roman 8 symbol set
E_C(s1p1v0s3b5T	Select Times Roman Bold 10 point FONT *

The FONT command will change all of the text following the sequence to boldface. This next PCL sequence changes the text following it to italic.

Command	Explanation
E_C&l0O	Select Landscape Orientation*
E_C(8U	select Roman 8 symbol set
E_C(s1p10v1s0b5T	Select Times Roman italic 10 point FONT *

To "turn off" the italic, and return the text to its roman typeface, enter this next PCL sequence so it precedes the text to be back in the original style.

Command	Explanation
E_C&l0O	Select Landscape Orientation*
E_C(8U	select Roman 8 symbol set
E_C(s1p10v0s0b5T	Select Times Roman 10 point FONT *

* See the Resident Fonts Table in the Programming Manual

```
I go, and it is done: the bell invites me.
Hear it not, Duncan, for it is a knell
That summons thee to heaven, or to hell.
<-&l0O<-(8U<-(slplv0s3b5T


                   Scene 2<-&l0O<-(8U<-(slpl0vls0b5T


Lady Macbeth enters
<-&l0O<-(8U<-(slpl0v0s0b5T
LADY M. That which hath made them drunk hath
made me bold;
```

Figure 4-16. PCL Sequence for bolding and italicizing subheads and fragments in text. Note that the sequence can be after the text fragment, or between paragraphs.

By inserting PCL sequences between paragraphs, you can easily control the shear, as well as the weight and the typeface of a font.

I go, and it is done: the bell invites me.
Hear it not, Duncan, for it is a knell
That summons thee to heaven, or to hell.

Scene 2

Lady Macbeth enters

LADY M. That which hath made them drunk hath
made me bold;

Figure 4-17. Printed text illustrating bold and italic text fragments in a document.

Dealing Effectively with Larger Fonts

The examples above illustrate the flexibility you can achieve just by changing the characteristics of a font. However, most word processors default to common line settings, usually either 6 or 8 lines per inch. This setting will accommodate 8 to 12 point type, but larger type will not fit on those line settings. In effect, you run out of line leading in order to accommodate the larger point type. The next example shows how to increase the line leading with a PCL command.

This sequence shows how to select a large size typeface for the title of your document, and adjust the leading to accommodate it.

Command	Explanation
E_C&l0O	Select Landscape Orientation*
E_C(8U	Select Roman 8 symbol set
E_C(s1p14.4v0s0b4T	Select Helvetica Bold 14.4 point FONT*
E_C&l11.3C	Set Line Spacing to 17 points

The FONT command will change all of the text following the sequence to the newly selected font. In order to adjust the line spacing, you must convert points (72nd of an inch) into 48ths of an inch, because that is the dimension PCL uses. Set the spacing to about 20% greater than the point size selected for the font. The 20% allows for easy reading of the text.

*   See the Resident Fonts Table in the Programming Manual

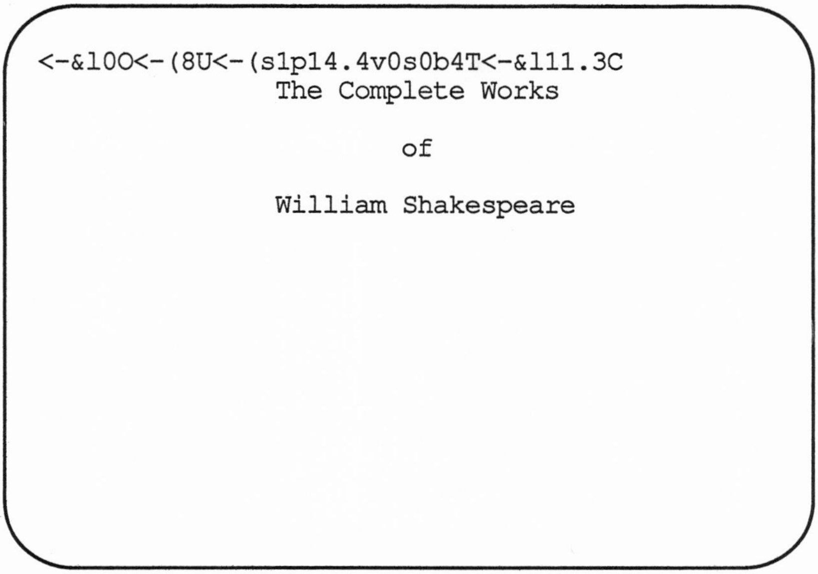

```
<-&l0O<-(8U<-(s1p14.4v0s0b4T<-&l11.3C
            The Complete Works

                    of

            William Shakespeare
```

Figure 4-18. PCL Sequence used to print larger type sizes, necessitating the adjustment of the leading, or line size.

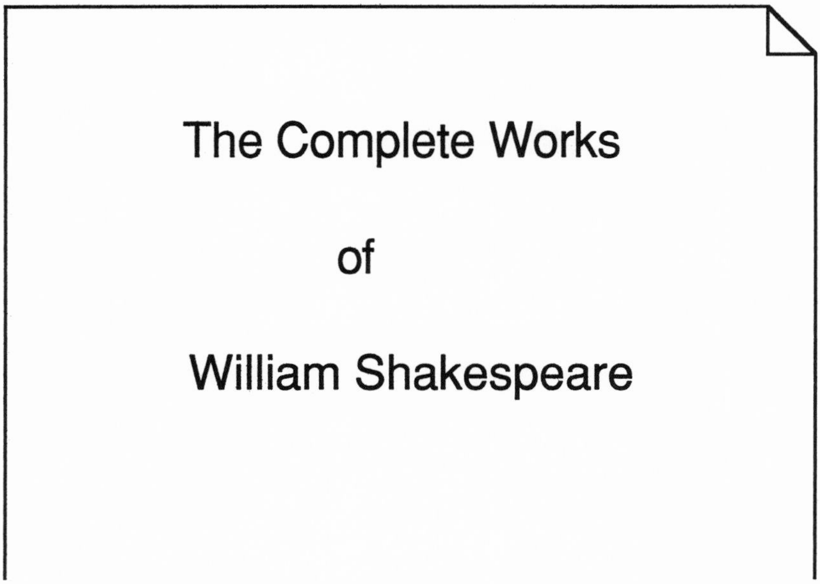

The Complete Works

of

William Shakespeare

Figure 4-19. Printed text in large type.

Chapter 5

Addressing Envelopes with Your Laser Printer

How many times have you printed a letter, then hand-addressed the envelope because you couldn't figure out how to do it on your laser printer? In this next example you'll see how easy it is to laserprint envelopes. Then, the next time you mail a business letter, what's on the outside of the envelope will look just as professional as what's on the inside.

Except for typing the text of the destination address, the process for printing an envelope is basically the same every time. Therefore if you set up the job once, you can use the process over and over for each newly addressed envelope.

You have a choice between two types of processes: an envelope macro, or an envelope template. A macro is essentially a short program consisting of a series of steps that the printer runs through each time you use the macro. A template, on the other hand, is like a pre-set format that you can then fill in with the appropriate address information. You can choose either process, or both of them, for an envelope printing method. Neither method is very difficult, nor is one significantly better than the other; the one you choose will be primarily a personal preference. Either way, you'll get the laser printer to print envelopes.

A MACRO FOR PRINTING ENVELOPES

In this example, you'll learn how to create and use an envelope macro on the Kyocera printer, using the Prescribe language. The macro is a convenient method that also illustrates the general capability of macros. The HP LaserJet also has a macro capability, and although it is more complex to use than the Kyocera, the general method presented in this example applies to the HP LaserJet as well.

Creating an Envelope Macro

The macro can be created in DOS, or in any word processing program. In DOS, be careful when entering each command because editing is difficult at best. If you find a mistake on a previous line, it's better to start over than to try to fix the mistake. By creating the macro in a word processing program, however, you can take advantage of the program's full editing capabilities. If you do decide to use the word processing program, save the file with the macro as an ASCII file, and give its filename the prefix ".MAC"

The macro is shown below. Before typing that macro into a file, however, you must make two decisions.

First, do your company's envelopes have a return address already printed on them? If they do then you won't want the laser printer to print a return address. In that case, *do not* include the first four TEXT commands that are already in the macro. But, if you plan to print on blank envelopes, *do* include those first four TEXT commands.

The second decision to make is how many lines to allow for the destination address. The number of TEXT% commands at the end of the macro determine the number of lines for the destination address. The macro now shows a total of six lines for the address. Add or delete the TEXT% commands to get the number of lines that you want.

If you're entering the macro using DOS, first enter the DOS command COPY CON ENVELOPE.MAC. This DOS command copies the contents of the screen to the file ENVELOPE.MAC. As you type, the contents of the screen are the macro commands that will be stored in ENVELOPE.MAC. If you're using a word processing program to enter the macro commands, do not type the DOS command. Instead, you'll use the program's standard save command to save the file as an ASCII file.

The macro shows the commands listed one per line, but you can also type the commands continuously without hitting the Return key. Here are the Prescribe commands to enter:

Command	Explanation
!R!	staRt Prescribe sequence
RES;	RESet printer options to default
DELM ENVELOPE;	DELete Macro named ENVELOPE
MCRO ENVELOPE;	create new MaCRO named ENVELOPE
CASS 0;	set paper CASSette to Manual Mode
FONT 17;	Select a landscape FONT of your choice*
SPSZ 2;	Set Paper SiZe to 2 — Business Envelope**
TEXT'',N;	create a blank TEXT line
TEXT'YOUR NAME',N;	Replace YOUR NAME with your real name
TEXT'ADDRESS',N;	Fill in your return address here
TEXT'CITY ST ZIP',N;	Add your City, State and Zip Code
STM 2;	Set Top Margin to 2 inches
SLM 4;	Set Left Margin to 4 inches
TEXT%1,N;	There 6 lines are variable text lines
TEXT%2,N;	for the destination address, which you
TEXT%3,N;	will supply when you call the macro.
TEXT%4,N;	
TEXT%5,N;	
TEXT%6,N;	
PAGE;	print the PAGE
RES;	RESet printer options to default
ENDM;	END the Macro definition
EXIT;	EXIT Prescribe sequence

* See the Resident Fonts Table in the Programming Manual

** See the Paper Sizes Table in the Programming Manual

If you entered the macro in DOS, now type ^Z to close the file. If you want to review the file in DOS, enter the DOS command TYPE ENVELOPE.MAC to list the file on the screen. If you have entered the macro in a word processing file, save the file as an ASCII file with the name ENVELOPE.MAC.

Downloading the Envelope Macro

As small programs, the macros can be loaded into the printer itself. Thus, to use the macro, you must first download it from the PC to the Kyocera printer. The downloading has to take place each time you turn on the printer, and before you try to print the envelopes. To download the macro from DOS, enter the command COPY ENVELOPE.MAC PRN. That command copies the file ENVELOPE.MAC from your PC's disk to the printer.

As a shortcut, you can also automate the process of downloading the macro by putting the COPY.ENVELOPE.MAC.PRN command in your PC's AUTOEXEC.BAT file. Then, each time you turn on the PC, the envelope macro is automatically downloaded and the printer will be ready to use.

After downloading is complete, the next step in printing the envelope is to "call" the macro and type the addressee.

Calling the Envelope Macro and Typing Addresses

To call the macro means to make it available for you to use. Calling a macro is like opening a file to work with it. You want to call the macro so you can type the destination addresses for the envelopes. You can call the macro from either DOS or from a word processing program. When calling the macro in DOS, enter the DOS command COPY CON PRN. That command copies the contents of the screen to the printer. If you are using a word processing program, skip the DOS command. Now, enter the following Prescribe commands:

Command	Explanation
!R!	staRt Prescribe sequence
CALL ENVELOPE,	CALL macro ENVELOPE
'Destination Name',	Enter the name of the destination,
'Address',	address, and up to 6 lines of text.
City, St ZIP';	The last line of text must end with a semicolon
EXIT;	EXIT Prescribe sequence

If you have entered this Prescribe sequence in DOS, enter ^Z to close the file. The printer will then print the envelopes. If you used a word processing program, type the sequence for opening the macro file, and then choose the command for printing. Insert your business envelope face up, and watch it come out the other side addressed and ready to go!

Figure 5-1. Printed business envelope with return and destination address.

CREATING AN ENVELOPE TEMPLATE

The other choice for printing envelopes is to use an envelope template. To create an envelope template, enter the Prescribe sequences below. Set the proper margin settings in the template for printing your envelopes automatically, and then save the template to disk. This process only has to be done once for each type of envelope you use.

From now on, each time you print a letter, follow these four simple steps.

1. Copy the mailing address from the top of your letter, using the copy text function for your word processor. If you don't have a copy text function, just skip this step. Sometimes the copy text function is called Copy and Paste. Its function is to save you the effort of having to re-type the address a second time for the envelope.

2. Next, open the envelope template (which you've already created) and insert the address you copied in step 1. If your program doesn't have the copy function, type in the address.

3. With the address entered correctly, choose the program's print command to print the envelope template to the laser printer.

4. Insert your envelope into the manual feeder on the laser printer, and the envelope will be printed. When you're done printing the envelope, close the envelope document *without* saving it. That way, it will be ready for you next time you want to print envelopes. (If you saved it, the template would contain the address you just typed.)

In this example you'll create an envelope document for a standard business envelope (approximately 4 inches high and 9 1/2 inches long). Of course, you can make other envelope templates if your envelopes are a different size.

Kyocera and Microsoft WORD

To create the envelope template, first clear the screen and create a new unnamed document. Next, enter the following Prescribe sequence. Each command can be on a separate line, because a command at the end of the sequence returns the cursor to its initial position.

Command	Explanation
!R!	staRt Prescribe sequence
RES;	RESet printer options to default
FONT 29;	Select a landscape FONT of your choice*
SPO L;	Set Page Orientation to Landscape
CASS 0;	set paper CASSette to Manual Mode
SPSZ 2;	Set Paper SiZe to 2 — Business Envelope**
STM 2;	Set Top Margin to 2 inches
SLM 4;	Set Left Margin to 4 inches
MAP 0,0;	Move Absolute Position of cursor to the top left corner of margins
EXIT;	EXIT Prescribe sequence

* See the Resident Fonts Table in the Programming Manual

** See the Paper Sizes Table in the Programming Manual

Next, enter the word "Address" on a new line, separated by one blank line above and below it. Right after "Address," enter this short Prescribe sequence to reset the Kyocera settings you've altered in the previous sequence in order to print the envelope.

Command	Explanation
!R!	staRt Prescribe sequence
RES;	RESet printer options to default
EXIT;	EXIT Prescribe sequence

Notice that the word "Address" is not actually part of the Prescribe sequence. It is merely a placeholder that you'll replace later with a real address. Therefore, to type in the real address, move the cursor to "Address," delete "Address," and type the real address or, if you have a copy and paste function, use it to delete "Address" and enter the real address.

```
!R!
RES;
FONT 29;
SPO L;
CASS 0;
SPSZ 2;
STM 2;
SLM 4;
MAP 0,0;
EXIT;
Kyocera Unison, Inc.
3165 Adeline Street
Berkeley, California 94703
!R!
RES;
EXIT;
```

Figure 5-2. Prescribe sequence for addressing business envelope in WORD.

Before You Print

WORD may send font commands on every text line, which will change the printing orientation unless specific drivers are used to print the envelope. For best results, use either the TTY or PLAIN drivers. If you embed the text of the addresses in Prescribe TEXT commands, you can also use the Kyocera Landscape orientation driver.

If you are using a Kyocera printer that has the manual feed foldout on the output side of the printer, fold it out now, so the envelope will not get bent as it exits the printer.

Test Your Work

Test your work by replacing the word "Address" with your own address. Print the envelope template to the laser printer. Next, insert a business envelope face up, with the top of the envelope facing the front side of the Kyocera, where the control panel is located. You may have to adjust the paper/envelope guides on the top of the paper cassette. When the envelope emerges from the printer, check the positioning of the address. If you want to make changes, modify the macro. Keep testing until the macro produces exactly the right addresses for your envelopes.

When you're satisfied with everything, save the template with some appropriate name such as "BUSENV." Now the business envelope template is ready for use the next time you write a letter.

Figure 5-3. Printed business envelope with destination address only.

Adding a Return Address

If you're not using preprinted business envelopes with your return address in the upper left hand corner, you'll want to add your return address directly to the envelope template. The address will print in the upper left corner of a plain business envelope.

To add a return address, you'll need to make changes to the Prescribe sequence for an envelope template. Those changes are shown in bold below.

Command	Explanation
!R!	staRt Prescribe sequence
RES;	RESet printer options to default
FONT 31;	**Select a smaller landscape FONT***
SPO L;	Set Page Orientation to Landscape
CASS 0;	set paper CASSette to Manual Mode
SPSZ 2;	Set Paper SiZe to 2 — Business Envelope**
EXIT;	**EXIT Prescribe sequence**
Your Name	
Your Address	
Your City, ST & ZIP	
!R!	**staRt Prescribe sequence**
FONT 29;	**Select a larger landscape FONT***
STM 2;	Set Top Margin to 2 inches

SLM 4;	Set Left Margin to 4 inches
MAP 0,0;	Move Absolute Position of cursor to 0, 0 — top, left corner of margins
EXIT;	EXIT Prescribe sequence

* See the Resident Fonts Table in the Programming Manual

```
!R!RES;FONT 31;SPO L;CASS 0;SPSZ 2;EXIT;
ABC Computers
100 Megabyte Drive
Binary, CA  99999
!R!FONT 29;STM 2;SLM 4;MAP 0,0;EXIT;
Kyocera Unison, Inc.
3165 Adeline Street
Berkeley, California 94703
!R!
RES;
EXIT;
```

Figure 5-4. Prescribe sequence for including return address on business envelope in WORD. The commands may be on the same line as shown, or on separate lines for readability.

As you can see, adding a return address to the envelope template is easy. Simply break the first sequence into two sequences by adding an additional EXIT command. Next, type in your name and address, and restart the rest of the sequence with the !R! command, followed by the destination address as before. If you'd like to use a smaller font on your return address, change the FONT command in the first sequence, and add a new FONT command to the second sequence, as shown above.

Now try printing this version of the envelope. When you've got it correct, save the template file with an appropriate name, such as BUSENVRA (RA for Return Address). Now you've got two business envelope templates to choose from — one for preprinted envelopes, and another for plain envelopes that will include your return address.

Figure 5-5. Printed business envelope with return and destination address.

Special Considerations

If you select a large font, you may need to adjust the left and top margins with the STM and SLM commands accordingly. Also, if you use a different-sized envelope, be sure to change the paper size with the SPSZ command to match the envelope as closely as possible. After you've changed and tested your commands, save the template with an appropriate name (being careful not to replace the original one). The template will then be available whenever you need it to print your envelopes.

Kyocera and MultiMate

To create the envelope template, first clear the screen and create a new unnamed document. Next, enter the following Prescribe sequence. Each command can be on a separate line, because a command at the end of the sequence returns the cursor to its initial position.

Command	Explanation
!R!	staRt Prescribe sequence
RES;	RESet printer options to default
FONT 29;	Select a landscape FONT of your choice*
SPO L;	Set Page Orientation to Landscape
CASS 0;	set paper CASSette to Manual Mode
SPSZ 2;	Set Paper SiZe to 2 — Business Envelope**
STM 2;	Set Top Margin to 2 inches
SLM 4;	Set Left Margin to 4 inches
MAP 0,0;	Move Absolute Position of cursor to the top left corner of margins
EXIT;	EXIT Prescribe sequence

* See the Resident Fonts Table in the Programming Manual

** See the Paper Sizes Table in the Programming Manual

Next, enter the word "Address" on a new line, separated by one blank line above and below it. Right after "Address," enter this short Prescribe sequence to reset the Kyocera settings you've altered in the previous sequence in order to print the envelope.

Command	Explanation
!R!	staRt Prescribe sequence
RES;	RESet printer options to default
EXIT;	EXIT Prescribe sequence

Notice that the word "Address" is not actually part of the Prescribe sequence. It is merely a placeholder that you'll replace later with a real address. Therefore, to type in the real address, move the cursor to "Address," delete "Address," and type the real address, or if you have a copy and paste function use it to delete "Address" and enter the real address.

```
!R!
RES;
FONT 29;
SPO L;
CASS 0;
SPSZ 2;
STM 2;
SLM 4;
MAP 0,0;
EXIT;
Kyocera Unison, Inc.
3165 Adeline Street
Berkeley, California 94703
!R!
RES;
EXIT;
```

Figure 5-6. Prescribe sequence for addressing business envelope in MultiMate.

Before You Print

For best results, use either the TTY, PLAIN, or DRAFT drivers. If you embed the text of the addresses in Prescribe TEXT commands, you can use the Kyocera Landscape driver such as KYOLAND as well.

If you are using a Kyocera printer that has the manual feed foldout on the output side of the printer, fold it out now, so the envelope will not get bent as it exits the printer.

Test Your Work

Test your work by replacing the word "Address" with your own address. Print the envelope template to the laser printer. Next, insert a business envelope face up, with the top of the envelope facing the front side of the Kyocera, where the control panel is located. You may have to adjust the paper/envelope guides on the top of the paper cassette. When the envelope emerges from the printer, check the positioning of the address. If you want to make changes, modify the macro. Keep testing until the macro produces exactly the right addresses for your envelopes.

When you're satisfied with everything, save the template with some appropriate name such as "BUSENV." Now the business envelope template is ready for use the next time you write a letter.

Figure 5-7. Printed business envelope with destination address only.

Adding a Return Address

If you're not using preprinted business envelopes with your return address in the upper left hand corner, you'll want to add your return address directly to the envelope template. The address will print in the upper left corner of a plain business envelope.

To add a return address, you'll need to make changes to the Prescribe sequence for an envelope template. Those changes are shown in bold below.

Command	Explanation
<u>Command</u>	<u>Explanation</u>
!R!	staRt Prescribe sequence
RES;	RESet printer options to default
FONT 31;	**Select a smaller landscape FONT***
SPO L;	Set Page Orientation to Landscape
CASS 0;	set paper CASSette to Manual Mode
SPSZ 2;	Set Paper SiZe to 2 — Business Envelope**
EXIT;	**EXIT Prescribe sequence**
Your Name	
Your Address	
Your City, ST & ZIP	
!R!	**staRt Prescribe sequence**
FONT 29;	**Select a larger landscape FONT***
STM 2;	Set Top Margin to 2 inches

SLM 4;	Set Left Margin to 4 inches
MAP 0,0;	Move Absolute Position of cursor to 0, 0 — top, left corner of margins
EXIT;	EXIT Prescribe sequence

* See the Resident Fonts Table in the Programming Manual

```
!R!RES;FONT 31;SPO L;CASS 0;SPSZ 2;EXIT;
ABC Computers
100 Megabyte Drive
Binary, CA  99999
!R!FONT 29;STM 2;SLM 4;MAP 0,0;EXIT;
Kyocera Unison, Inc.
3165 Adeline Street
Berkeley, California 94703
!R!
RES;
EXIT;
```

Figure 5-8. Prescribe sequence for including return address on business envelope in MultiMate. The commands may be on the same line as shown, or on separate lines for readability.

As you can see, adding a return address to the envelope template is easy. Simply break the first sequence into two sequences by adding an additional EXIT command. Next, type in your name and address, and restart the rest of the sequence with the !R! command, followed by the destination address as before. If you'd like to use a smaller font on your return address, change the FONT command in the first sequence, and add a new FONT command to the second sequence, as shown above.

Now try printing this version of the envelope. When you've got it correct, save the template file with an appropriate name, such as BUSENVRA (RA for Return Address). Now you've got two business envelope templates to choose from — one for preprinted envelopes, and another for plain envelopes that will include your return address.

Figure 5-9. Printed business envelope with return and destination address.

Special Considerations

If you select a large font, you may need to adjust the left and top margins with the STM and SLM commands accordingly. Also, if you use a different-sized envelope, be sure to change the paper size with the SPSZ command to match the envelope as closely as possible. After you've changed and tested your commands, save the template with an appropriate name (being careful not to replace the original one). The template will then be available whenever you need it to print your envelopes.

Kyocera and WordStar

To create the envelope template, first clear the screen and create a new unnamed document. Next, enter the following Prescribe sequence. Each command can be on a separate line, because a command at the end of the sequence returns the cursor to its initial position.

Command	Explanation
!R!	staRt Prescribe sequence
RES;	RESet printer options to default
FONT 29;	Select a landscape FONT of your choice*
SPO L;	Set Page Orientation to Landscape
CASS 0;	set paper CASSette to Manual Mode
SPSZ 2;	Set Paper SiZe to 2 — Business Envelope**
STM 2;	Set Top Margin to 2 inches
SLM 4;	Set Left Margin to 4 inches
MAP 0,0;	Move Absolute Position of cursor to the top left corner of margins
EXIT;	EXIT Prescribe sequence

* See the Resident Fonts Table in the Programming Manual
** See the Paper Sizes Table in the Programming Manual

Next, enter the word "Address" on a new line, separated by one blank line above and below it. Right after "Address," enter this short Prescribe sequence to reset the Kyocera settings you've altered in the previous sequence in order to print the envelope.

Command	Explanation
!R!	staRt Prescribe sequence
RES;	RESet printer options to default
EXIT;	EXIT Prescribe sequence

Notice that the word "Address" is not actually part of the Prescribe sequence. It is merely a placeholder that you'll replace later with a real address. Therefore, to type in the real address, move the cursor to "Address," delete "Address," and type the real address, or if you have a copy and paste function use it to delete "Address" and enter the real address.

```
!R!
RES;
FONT 29;
SPO L;
CASS 0;
SPSZ 2;
STM 2;
SLM 4;
MAP 0,0;
EXIT;
Kyocera Unison, Inc.
3165 Adeline Street
Berkeley, California 94703
!R!
RES;
EXIT;
```

Figure 5-10. Prescribe sequence for addressing business envelope in WordStar.

Before You Print

For best results, use the DRAFT driver. The .op command may be necessary to avoid page numbering.

If you are using a Kyocera printer that has the manual feed foldout on the output side of the printer, fold it out now, so the envelope will not get bent as it exits the printer.

Test Your Work

Test your work by replacing the word "Address" with your own address. Print the envelope template to the laser printer. Next, insert a business envelope face up, with the top of the envelope facing the front side of the Kyocera, where the control panel is located. You may have to adjust the paper/envelope guides on the top of the paper cassette. When the envelope emerges from the printer, check the positioning of the address. If you want to make changes, modify the macro. Keep testing until the macro produces exactly the right addresses for your envelopes.

When you're satisfied with everything, save the template with some appropriate name such as "BUSENV." Now the business envelope template is ready for use the next time you write a letter.

Kyocera Unison, Inc.
3165 Adeline Street
Berkeley, California 94703

Figure 5-11. Printed business envelope with destination address only.

Adding a Return Address

If you're not using preprinted business envelopes with your return address in the upper left hand corner, you'll want to add your return address directly to the envelope template. The address will print in the upper left corner of a plain business envelope.

To add a return address, you'll need to make changes to the Prescribe sequence for an envelope template. Those changes are shown in bold below.

Command	Explanation
!R!	staRt Prescribe sequence
RES;	RESet printer options to default
FONT 31;	**Select a smaller landscape FONT***
SPO L;	Set Page Orientation to Landscape
CASS 0;	set paper CASSette to Manual Mode
SPSZ 2;	Set Paper SiZe to 2 — Business Envelope**
EXIT;	**EXIT Prescribe sequence**
Your Name	
Your Address	
Your City, ST & ZIP	

!R!	**staRt Prescribe sequence**
FONT 29;	**Select a larger landscape FONT***
STM 2;	Set Top Margin to 2 inches
SLM 4;	Set Left Margin to 4 inches
MAP 0,0;	Move Absolute Position of cursor to 0, 0 — top, left corner of margins
EXIT;	EXIT Prescribe sequence

*   See the Resident Fonts Table in the Programming Manual

```
!R!RES;FONT 31;SPO L;CASS 0;SPSZ 2;EXIT;
ABC Computers
100 Megabyte Drive
Binary, CA  99999
!R!FONT 29;STM 2;SLM 4;MAP 0,0;EXIT;
Kyocera Unison, Inc.
3165 Adeline Street
Berkeley, California 94703
!R!
RES;
EXIT;
```

Figure 5-12. Prescribe sequence for including return address on business envelope in WordStar. The commands may be on the same line as shown, or on separate lines for readability.

As you can see, adding a return address to the envelope template is easy. Simply break the first sequence into two sequences by adding an additional EXIT command. Next, type in your name and address, and restart the rest of the sequence with the !R! command, followed by the destination address as before. If you'd like to use a smaller font on your return address, change the FONT command in the first sequence, and add a new FONT command to the second sequence, as shown above.

Now try printing this version of the envelope. When you've got it correct, save the template file with an appropriate name, such as BUSENVRA. (RA for Return Address). Now you've got two business envelope templates to choose from — one for preprinted envelopes, and another for plain envelopes that will include your return address.

```
ABC Computers
100 Megabyte Drive
Binary, CA  99999


                         Kyocera Unison, Inc.
                         3165  Adeline  Street
                         Berkeley,  California  94703
```

Figure 5-13. Printed business envelope with return and destination address.

Special Considerations

If you select a large font, you may need to adjust the left and top margins with the STM and SLM commands accordingly. Also, if you use a different-sized envelope, be sure to change the paper size with the SPSZ command to match the envelope as closely as possible. After you've changed and tested your commands, save the template with an appropriate name (being careful not to replace the original one). The template will then be available whenever you need it to print your envelopes.

HP LaserJet and Microsoft WORD

To create the envelope template, first clear the window and create a new unnamed document. Next, enter the following PCL sequence (each command can be on a separate line):

Command	Explanation
E_CE	Reset printer options to default
E_C&l1O	Set page orientation to landscape
E_C&l24E	Set top margin to 24 lines
E_C&l3H	Set paper cassette to manual mode

Next, enter the word "Address" on a separate line, separated by one blank line above and below it. Notice that "Address" is not actually part of the PCL sequence. It is merely a placeholder which you'll replace later with a real address each time you print. If you have a copy and paste function in your word processor, you can use it. If not, you can just type in the address. In either case, be sure to delete the word "Address" when you're using the template.

Right after "Address," enter this short PCL sequence to reset the HP LaserJet settings you've altered in the previous sequence in order to print the envelope.

Command	Explanation
E_CE	Reset printer options to default

```
<-E<-&l1O<-&l24E<-&l3H
Kyocera Unison, Inc.
3165 Adeline Street
Berkeley, California 94703
<-E
```

Figure 5-14. PCL sequence for addressing business envelope in WORD.

Before You Print

For best results, use the PLAIN or TTY driver. If you use the HPLASLAN driver, you'll get a blank page before you insert the envelope. If you are using a printer that has the manual feed foldout on the output side of the printer, fold it out now, so the envelope will not get bent as it exits the printer.

Set your margins to the following settings:

Top = 0"
Bottom = 0"
Left = 6"
Right = .5"
Page Length = 11"
Width = 8.5"

Test Your Work

Now, test your work by replacing "Address" with your own address in the same place "Address" was located. Print the envelope template to the laser printer. Next, insert a business envelope into the printer face up, with the top of the envelope facing to the left. You may have to adjust the paper/envelope guides on the top of the paper cassette.

If the address came out correctly on your envelope, that's all you have to do. If not, just adjust the settings in the PCL commands, or move the paper guides. When you're satisfied everything is working correctly, save the file with an appropriate name such as "BUSENV." Now the business envelope template is ready for use next time you write a letter.

Kyocera Unison, Inc.
3165 Adeline Street
Berkeley, California 94703

Figure 5-15. Printed business envelope with destination address only.

Adding a Return Address

The example above assumes that you're using business envelopes with your return address preprinted in the upper left hand corner. In this next example you'll include your return address in the envelope template, so it will print properly on a plain envelope.

This example is only slightly different from the previous example, so if you want to modify the previous example rather than starting from scratch, you can.

Command	Explanation
E_CE	Reset printer options to default
E_C&l1O	Set page orientation to landscape
E_C&l14E	Set top margin to 14 lines
E_C&l3H	Set paper cassette to manual mode
Your Name	
Your Address	
Your City, ST & ZIP	

The first line of the return address should be typed directly after the last PCL command, before entering a carriage return. Finish entering the return address as you normally would. Next, skip 8 lines, set a tab at 4 inches, and type in the destination address. Finally, change your left margin to 6 inches.

```
<-E<-&l1O<-&l14E<-&l3HABC Computers
100 Megabyte Drive
Binary, CA  99999




                        Kyocera Unison, Inc.
                        3165 Adeline Street
                        Berkeley, California 94703
                        <-E
```

Figure 5-16. PCL sequence for including return address on business envelope in WORD.

Test Your Work

Now try printing this version of the envelope. When it's correct, be sure to save the file with an appropriate name, such as BUSENVRA (RA for Return Address). Now you've got two business envelope templates to choose from — one for preprinted envelopes, and another for plain envelopes.

Figure 5-17. Printed business envelope with return and destination address.

Special Considerations

If you want to select fonts, you will need to add the font commands accordingly. Also, if you use a different-sized envelope, you may need to adjust the number of lines to match the envelope's size. After you've changed and tested your commands, be sure to save the template with an appropriate name (being careful not to replace the original one), so it will be available whenever you need it to print your envelopes.

HP LaserJet and MultiMate

To create the envelope template, first clear the window and create a new unnamed document. Next, enter the following PCL sequence (each command can be on a separate line):

Command	Explanation
E_CE	Reset printer options to default
E_C&l1O	Set page orientation to landscape
E_C&l24E	Set top margin to 24 lines
E_C&l3H	Set paper cassette to manual mode

Next, enter the word "Address" on a separate line, separated by one blank line above and below. Notice that "Address" is not actually part of the PCL sequence. It is merely a placeholder which you'll replace later with a real address each time you print. If you have a copy and paste function in your word processor, you can use it. If not, you can just type in the address. In either case, be sure to delete the word "Address" when you're using the template.

Right after "Address," enter this short PCL sequence to reset the HP LaserJet settings you've altered in the previous sequence in order to print the envelope.

Command	Explanation
E_CE	Reset printer options to default

```
<-E<-&l1O<-&l24E<-&l3H
Kyocera Unison, Inc.
3165 Adeline Street
Berkeley, California 94703
<-E
```

Figure 5-18. PCL sequence for addressing business envelope in MultiMate.

Before You Print

Some setup is required in MultiMate before you can print envelopes using this example. First, you'll need to modify a PAT (Printer Action Table) named LJETENV. Enter the hexadecimal sequence "1B266C3368314F" in the Printer Initialization field (it's the first field on the Table). Save this table with a new name, such as LJENV. This will set the printer for envelopes and landscape mode. For complete step-by-step instructions, see the *MultiMate Printer Guide*. Next, when you start the new file, set the number of lines per page to 45 using the Modify Document Defaults Menu.

If you are using a printer that has the manual feed foldout on the output side of the printer, fold it out now, so the envelope will not get bent as it exits the printer.

Test Your Work

Now, test your work by replacing "Address" with your own address in the same place "Address" was located. Print the envelope template to the laser printer. Next, insert a business envelope into the printer face up, with the top of the envelope facing to the left. You may have to adjust the paper/envelope guides on the top of the paper cassette.

If the address came out correctly on your envelope, that's all you have to do. If not, just adjust the settings in the PCL commands, or move the paper guides. When you're satisfied everything is working correctly, save the file with an appropriate name such as "BUSENV." Now the business envelope template is ready for use next time you write a letter.

Kyocera Unison, Inc.
3165 Adeline Street
Berkeley, California 94703

Figure 5-19. Printed business envelope with destination address only.

Adding a Return Address

The example above assumes that you're using business envelopes with your return address preprinted in the upper left hand corner. In this next example you'll include your return address in the envelope template, so it will print properly on a plain envelope.

This example is only slightly different from the previous example, so you can modify it rather than starting from scratch.

Command	Explanation
E_CE	Reset printer options to default
E_C&l1O	Set page orientation to landscape
E_C&l14E	Set top margin to 14 lines
E_C&l3H	Set paper cassette to manual mode
Your Name	
Your Address	
Your City, ST & ZIP	

The first line of the return address should be typed directly after the last PCL command, before entering a carriage return. Finish entering the return address as you normally would. Next, skip 8 lines, set a tab at 4 inches, and type in the destination address. Finally, set your left margin to 6 inches.

```
<-E<-&l1O<-&l14E<-&l3HABC Computers
100 Megabyte Drive
Binary, CA  99999




                    Kyocera Unison, Inc.
                    3165 Adeline Street
                    Berkeley, California 94703
                    <-E
```

Figure 5-20. PCL sequence for including return address on business envelope in Multimate.

Test Your Work

Now try printing this version of the envelope document. When it's correct, save the file with an appropriate name, such as BUSENVRA (RA for Return Address). Now you've got two business envelope documents to choose from — one for preprinted envelopes, and another for plain envelopes.

Figure 5-21. Printed business envelope with return and destination address.

Special Considerations

If you want to select fonts, you will need to add the font commands accordingly. Also, if you use a different-sized envelope, you may need to adjust the number of lines to match the envelope's size. After you've changed and tested your commands, save the template with an appropriate name (being careful not to replace the original one), so it will be available whenever you need it to print your envelopes.

HP LaserJet and WordStar

To create the envelope template, first clear the window and create a new unnamed document. Next, enter the following PCL sequence (each command can be on a separate line):

Command	Explanation
E$_C$E	Reset printer options to default
E$_C$&l1O	Set page orientation to landscape
E$_C$&l3H	Set paper cassette to manual mode
.mt 25	Set top margin to 25 lines
.op	no page numbers
.lm 50	set left margin to 50 columns

Notice that the last 3 commands are not PCL commands; they are WordStar commands. Next, enter the word "Address" on a separate line, separated by one blank line above and below. Notice that "Address" is not actually part of the PCL sequence. It is merely a placeholder which you'll replace later with a real address each time you print. If you have a copy and paste function in your word processor, you can use it. If not, you can just type in the address. In either case, be sure to delete the word "Address" when you're using the template.

Right after "Address," enter this short PCL sequence to reset the HP LaserJet settings you've altered in the previous sequence in order to print the envelope.

Command	Explanation
E$_C$E	Reset printer options to default

```
<-E<-&l1O<-&l24E<-&l3H
Kyocera Unison, Inc.
3165 Adeline Street
Berkeley, California 94703
<-E
```

Figure 5-22. PCL sequence for addressing business envelope in WordStar.

Before You Print

For best results, use the DRAFT driver. If you are using a printer that has the manual feed foldout on the output side of the printer, fold it out now, so the envelope will not get bent as it exits the printer.

Test Your Work

Now, test your work by replacing "Address" with your own address in the same place "Address" was located. Print the envelope template to the laser printer. Next, insert a business envelope into the printer face up, with the top of the envelope facing to the left. You may have to adjust the paper/envelope guides on the top of the paper cassette.

If the address came out correctly on your envelope, that's all you have to do. If not, just adjust the settings in the PCL commands, or move the paper guides. When you're satisfied everything is working correctly, save the file with an appropriate name such as "BUSENV." Now the business envelope template is ready for use next time you write a letter.

Kyocera Unison, Inc.
3165 Adeline Street
Berkeley, California 94703

Figure 5-23. Printed business envelope with destination address only.

Adding a Return Address

The example above assumes that you're using business envelopes with your return address preprinted in the upper left hand corner. In this next example you'll include your return address in the envelope template, so it will print properly on a plain envelope.

This example is only slightly different from the previous example, so you can modify it rather than starting from scratch.

Command	Explanation
E_CE	Reset printer options to default
E_C&l1O	Set page orientation to landscape
E_C&l3H	Set paper cassette to manual mode
.mt 14	Set top margin to 14 lines
.op	no page numbers
Your Name	
Your Address	
Your City, ST & ZIP	

Notice that the last two commands are not PCL commands; they are WordStar commands. Enter the return address as you normally would. Next, skip 8 lines, set a tab at 4 inches, and type in the destination address.

```
<-E<-&l1O<-&l14E<-&l3HABC Computers
100 Megabyte Drive
Binary, CA  99999




                              Kyocera Unison, Inc.
                              3165 Adeline Street
                              Berkeley, California 94703
                              <-E
```

Figure 5-24. PCL sequence for including return address on business envelope in WordStar.

Test Your Work

Now try printing this version of the envelope document. When it's correct, save it with an appropriate name, such as BUSENVRA (RA for Return Address). Now you've got two business envelope documents to choose from — one for preprinted envelopes, and another for plain envelopes.

Figure 5-25. Printed business envelope with return and destination address.

Special Considerations

If you want to select fonts, you will need to add the font commands accordingly. Also, if you use a different-sized envelope, you may need to adjust the number of lines to match the envelope's size. After you've changed and tested your commands, save the template with an appropriate name (being careful not to replace the original one), so it will be available whenever you need it to print your envelopes.

Chapter 6

Creating Transparencies for Business Presentations

Business presentations are often the most difficult but most important part of a job. To communicate effectively with customers, fellow workers, and management literally demands a high quality presentation, because even the best information suffers when presented poorly. On the other hand, a quality presentation not only gives your image a professional polish, it also helps to get the response you want from your audience—whether it be a customer agreeing to a sale, or a manager accepting an innovative idea. In short, how you say something is almost as important as what you say. And that's where quality, laser-printed transparencies can make the difference.

Very likely, this single issue — the requirement for the quality presentation of business information — has contributed more to the sales of laser printers than any other issue. In this next example, you'll see how to use the features and fonts in your laser printer to create presentation-quality transparencies.

Producing a business presentation is not usually a quick, one-step process. Like any creative endeavor, producing a business presentation is an iterative process consisting of drafts, working copies, and editorial changes until the final presentation is just right. Because of this process, you'll normally want to print working copies of your presentation pages on regular paper instead of transparencies. You can then vary the layout on the page, adjust the height and style of fonts you've chosen for text, and move words and graphics around for maximum effectiveness. Then, once the presentation is finalized and ready to be printed, you can print it on transparencies.

When printing your final presentation, print an extra copy on paper. Use the paper copies to separate the transparencies so you can read the slides more easily. The paper also helps eliminate the static cling that often accompanies transparencies. If you want to make speaking notes for the presentation, use the paper copies for that purpose too.

The following example shows how to choose fonts, styles, and sizes for your presentation slides. Use the same methods in the example to create your own presentation and you'll soon see why so many people have purchased laser printers for printing business presentations.

KYOCERA AND MICROSOFT WORD

Presentation transparencies are displayed with an overhead projector, often in a large room and to a large audience. Therefore, you'll want to use a large, crisp font that reads well from all corners of the room. Part of this example shows how to build your own dynamic font to supplement the Kyocera's built-in fonts. Those built-in fonts are only intended for letters and other documents, not for overhead transparencies.

Here is the sequence you'll use for a bullet chart. The bullet symbol is the asterisk (*). On the chart the title is centered in a larger font, and each bullet point is left-justified in somewhat smaller type.

Command	Explanation
!R!	staRt Prescribe sequence
RES;	RESet printer options to default
SPO L;	Set Page Orientation to Landscape
GENF 201,'DYNAMIC1',.5,32,126,32,1,0,3,0,0,0;	
GENF 202,'DYNAMIC1',.33,32,126,32,1,0,3,0,0,0;	
	GENerate Font dynamically
FONT 201;	Select the half-inch FONT just generated
MAP 5.25,2;	Move Absolute Position of cursor 5.25 inches right and 2 inches down the page
CTXT 'Super-Co 1st Quarter Notables';	print Centered TeXT string
FONT 202;	Select the one-third inch FONT just generated
MAP 2,3;	Move Absolute Position of cursor 2 inches right and 3 inches down
TEXT '* Revenue is up by 37%';	print TEXT string
MAP 2,4;	Move Absolute Position of cursor 2 inches right and 4 inches down
TEXT '* Net Profit has risen by 41%';	print TEXT string
MAP 2,5;	Move Absolute Position of cursor 2 inches right and 5 inches down
TEXT '* Employee count is up only 14%';	print TEXT string
EXIT;	EXIT the Prescribe sequence

```
!R!
RES;
SPO L;
GENF 201,'DYNAMIC1',.5,32,126,32,1,0,3,0,0,0;
GENF 202,'DYNAMIC1',.33,32,126,32,1,0,3,0,0,0;
FONT 201;
MAP 5.25,2;
CTXT 'Super-Co 1st Quarter Notables';
FONT 202;
MAP 2,3;
TEXT '*  Revenue is up by 37%';
MAP 2,4;
TEXT '*  Net Profit has risen by 41%';
MAP 2,5;
TEXT '*  Employee count is up only 14%';
EXIT;
```

Figure 6-1. Prescribe Sequence for creating a business presentation in WORD. Use this sample as a guide for multiple-page presentations as well.

Unlike most of the other examples in this book, this one uses no embedded text for the word processing program. The text to be printed is all in Prescribe text commands. In some ways, control of the page is simpler using Prescribe commands because you're not trying to get two programs—the word processor and the Prescribe language—to work together.

In the sequence, the font-generating command (GENF) appears to be the most foreboding because of its string of numbers. Those numbers are options for the type of font you're generating. For instance, the first number (201) is simply the number of the font you're creating, and the .5 after the font name sets the height of the font. Each of the other numbers has a similar special meaning. To understand the GENF command and its options, refer to the *Prescribe Programmer's Reference Manual*.

Also notice that the horizontal coordinate of the MAP command is 5.25, not 5.5, which would evenly divide an 11-inch wide sheet of paper along its horizontal axis (in landscape mode). But 5.25 on each side of the center only adds up to 10.5 inches, and seemingly puts the cursor a half inch shy of the center. The reason to use 5.25 is due to the way the Kyocera aligns the

printer for the MAP command. The printer starts at the left margin of the print area, which is in 5 centimeters from the physical left edge of the paper. To compensate for that 5 cm, .25 inches is subtracted from the horizontal coordinate of the MAP command, to yield 5.25.

The CTXT command prints the headline text in the 201 font, centered at the location of the cursor. The next portion of the sequence selects the second generated font (202), and then repositions the cursor to print the text for the first bullet. Each TEXT command prints a line on the bullet chart.

By using this example you'll be able to print the title of each page in 1/2-inch text using FONT 201, and the bullet items in 1/3-inch text using FONT 202. Of course, you can make adjustments to the font sizes and line spacing for your own transparencies.

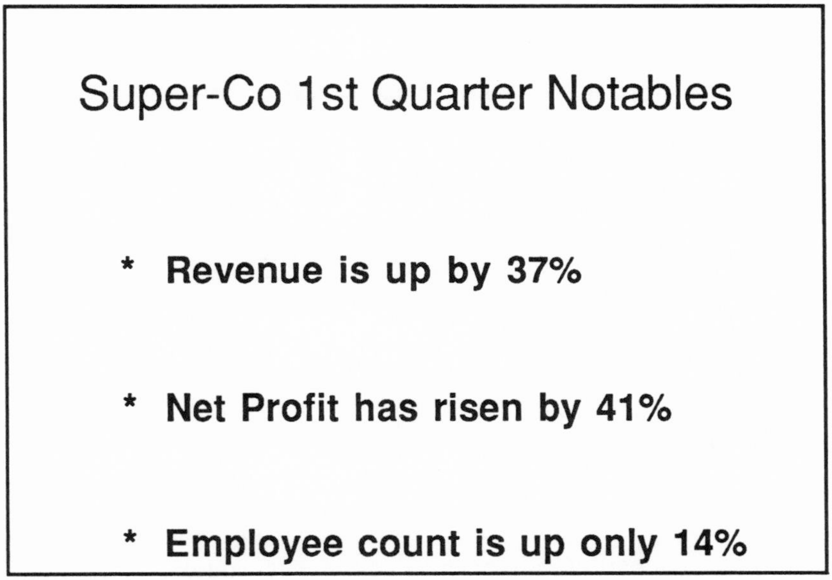

Super-Co 1st Quarter Notables

* **Revenue is up by 37%**

* **Net Profit has risen by 41%**

* **Employee count is up only 14%**

Figure 6-2. Business presentation printed in landscape orientation on transparency sheet for overhead projectors.

Brightening Up Your Presentation

Often, a business presentation can get boring, especially if the slides are all words with no graphic elements to add visual interest. To improve the look of your overheads, place a border around the entire page by using the BOX command. Use the examples in Chapter 10 of this book to see how to draw borders around the entire slide, or around portions of text on the slide. You use the Prescribe BOX command to draw the borders.

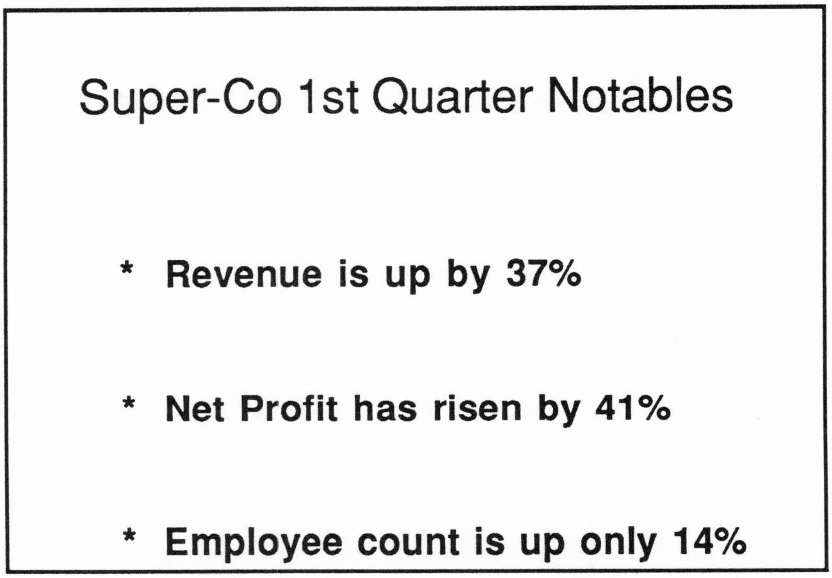

Super-Co 1st Quarter Notables

* **Revenue is up by 37%**

* **Net Profit has risen by 41%**

* **Employee count is up only 14%**

Figure 6-3. Spruce up your presentation with borders (see Chapter 10 for examples).

Before You Print

Because the text and formatting controls for the presentation pages are entirely in Prescribe commands, you don't have to make any changes in the word processing program prior to printing. The printing functions of the WORD program won't alter the pages at all. Usually, the worst that can happen is an occasional blank page caused by the program repaginating pages of commands that are more than one page in length. Another benefit of using only Prescribe commands is that you don't have to be concerned with the type of printer driver program installed for the word processing program.

Multi-Page Considerations

Of course, business presentations are rarely one page long. In order to print multiple presentation pages, you add the PAGE command between the sequences for each page in your presentation. Then, for each page, repeat the commands that start with the first font selection right after the GENF commands.

So you don't have to retype all of the commands, use your word processing program's copy-and-paste function to copy the relevant commands, and insert them just prior to the EXIT command. Remember that the EXIT command must be the last command in the sequence. Using the copy-and-paste technique, you can create as many pages as you need, and then just edit the text for each page.

The benefit of duplicating the information page-by-page in this manner is two-fold: first, copying correct sequences avoids typographical errors; and second, you can be sure that the formats of subsequent slides are the same as the first one. Thus you can duplicate as many as you need and then edit the text for each new page, concentrating on the message content and not on the mechanics of getting it on the page.

In fact, as you develop more presentations with Prescribe, save the sequences you use to create the slides. You can then re-use those sequences for later presentations by editing the text in the TEXT commands. Eventually, you'll have a library of slide examples and corresponding sequences for creating captivating presentations.

KYOCERA AND MULTIMATE

Presentation transparencies are displayed with an overhead projector, often in a large room and to a large audience. Therefore, you'll want to use a large, crisp font that reads well from all corners of the room. Part of this example shows how to build your own dynamic font to supplement the Kyocera's built-in fonts. Those built-in fonts are only intended for letters and other documents, not for overhead transparencies.

Here is the sequence you'll use for a bullet chart. The bullet symbol is the asterisk (*). On the chart the title is centered in a larger font, and each bullet point is left-justified in somewhat smaller type.

Command	Explanation
!R!	staRt Prescribe sequence
RES;	RESet printer options to default
SPO L;	Set Page to Landscape
GENF 201,'DYNAMIC1',.5,32,126,32,1,0,3,0,0,0;	
GENF 202,'DYNAMIC1',.33,32,126,32,1,0,3,0,0,0;	
	GENerate Font dynamically
FONT 201;	Select the half-inch FONT just generated
MAP 5.25,2;	Move Absolute Position of cursor 5.25 inches right and 2 inches down the page
CTXT 'Super-Co 1st Quarter Notables';	print Centered TeXT string
FONT 202;	Select the one-third inch FONT just generated
MAP 2,3;	Move Absolute Position of cursor 2 inches right and 3 inches down
TEXT '* Revenue is up by 37%';	print TEXT string
MAP 2,4;	Move Absolute Position of cursor 2 inches right and 4 inches down
TEXT '* Net Profit has risen by 41%';	print TEXT string
MAP 2,5;	Move Absolute Position of cursor 2 inches right and 5 inches down
TEXT '* Employee count is up only 14%';	print TEXT string
EXIT;	EXIT the Prescribe sequence

```
!R!
RES;
SPO L;
GENF 201,'DYNAMIC1',.5,32,126,32,1,0,3,0,0,0;
GENF 202,'DYNAMIC1',.33,32,126,32,1,0,3,0,0,0;
FONT 201;
MAP 5.25,2;
CTXT 'Super-Co 1st Quarter Notables';
FONT 202;
MAP 2,3;
TEXT '*  Revenue is up by 37%';
MAP 2,4;
TEXT '*  Net Profit has risen by 41%';
MAP 2,5;
TEXT '*  Employee count is up only 14%';
EXIT;
```

Figure 6-4. Prescribe Sequence for creating a business presentation in MultiMate. Use this sample as a guide for multiple-page presentations as well.

Unlike most of the other examples in this book, this one uses no embedded text for the word processing program. The text to be printed is all in Prescribe text commands. In some ways, control of the page is simpler using Prescribe commands because you're not trying to get two programs—the word processor and the Prescribe language—to work together.

In the sequence, the font-generating command (GENF) appears to be the most foreboding because of its string of numbers. Those numbers are options for the type of font you're generating. For instance, the first number (201) is simply the number of the font you're creating, and the .5 after the font name sets the height of the font. Each of the other numbers has a similar special meaning. To understand the GENF command and its options, refer to the *Prescribe Programmer's Reference Manual.*

Also notice that the horizontal coordinate of the MAP command is 5.25, not 5.5, which would evenly divide an 11-inch wide sheet of paper along its horizontal axis (in landscape mode). But 5.25 on each side of the center only adds up to 10.5 inches, and seemingly puts the cursor a half inch shy of the center. The reason to use 5.25 is due to the way the Kyocera aligns the

printer for the MAP command. The printer starts at the left margin of the print area, which is in 5 centimeters from the physical left edge of the paper. To compensate for that 5 cm, .25 inches is subtracted from the horizontal coordinate of the MAP command, to yield 5.25.

The CTXT command prints the headline text in the 201 font, centered at the location of the cursor. The next portion of the sequence selects the second generated font (202), and then repositions the cursor to print the text for the first bullet. Each TEXT command prints a line on the bullet chart.

By using this example you'll be able to print the title of each page in 1/2-inch text using FONT 201, and the bullet items in 1/3-inch text using FONT 202. Of course, you can make adjustments to the font sizes and line spacing for your own transparencies.

Super-Co 1st Quarter Notables

* **Revenue is up by 37%**

* **Net Profit has risen by 41%**

* **Employee count is up only 14%**

Figure 6-5. Business presentation printed in landscape orientation on transparency sheet for overhead projectors.

Brightening Up Your Presentation

Often, a business presentation can get boring, especially if the slides are all words with no graphic elements to add visual interest. To improve the look of your overheads, place a border around the entire page by using the BOX command. Use the examples in Chapter 10 of this book to see how to draw borders around the entire slide, or around portions of text on the slide. You use the Prescribe BOX command to draw the borders.

Super-Co 1st Quarter Notables

* **Revenue is up by 37%**

* **Net Profit has risen by 41%**

* **Employee count is up only 14%**

Figure 6-6. Spruce up your presentation with borders (see Chapter 10 for examples).

Before You Print

Because the text and formatting controls for the presentation pages are entirely in Prescribe commands, you don't have to make any changes in the word processing program prior to printing. The printing functions of the MultiMate program won't alter the pages at all. Usually, the worst that can happen is an occasional blank page caused by the program repaginating pages of commands that are more than one page in length. Another benefit of using only Prescribe commands is that you don't have to be concerned with the type of printer driver program installed for the word processing program.

Multi-Page Considerations

Of course, business presentations are rarely one page long. In order to print multiple presentation pages, you add the PAGE command between the sequences for each page in your presentation. Then, for each page, repeat the commands that start with the first font selection right after the GENF commands.

So you don't have to retype all of the commands, use your word processing program's copy-and-paste function to copy the relevant commands, and insert them just prior to the EXIT command. Remember that the EXIT command must be the last command in the sequence. Using the copy-and-paste technique, you can create as many pages as you need, and then just edit the text for each page.

The benefit of duplicating the information page-by-page in this manner is two-fold: first, copying correct sequences avoids typographical errors; and second, you can be sure that the formats of subsequent slides are the same as the first one. Thus you can duplicate as many as you need and then edit the text for each new page, concentrating on the message content and not on the mechanics of getting it on the page.

In fact, as you develop more presentations with Prescribe, save the sequences you use to create the slides. You can then re-use those sequences for later presentations by editing the text in the TEXT commands. Eventually, you'll have a library of slide examples and corresponding sequences for creating captivating presentations.

KYOCERA AND WORDSTAR

Presentation transparencies are displayed with an overhead projector, often in a large room and to a large audience. Therefore, you'll want to use a large, crisp font that reads well from all corners of the room. Part of this example shows how to build your own dynamic font to supplement the Kyocera's built-in fonts. Those built-in fonts are only intended for letters and other documents, not for overhead transparencies.

Here is the sequence you'll use for a bullet chart. The bullet symbol is the asterisk (*). On the chart the title is centered in a larger font, and each bullet point is left-justified in somewhat smaller type.

Command	Explanation
!R!	staRt Prescribe sequence
RES;	RESet printer options to default
SPO L;	Set Page Orientation to Landscape
GENF 201,'DYNAMIC1',.5,32,126,32,1,0,3,0,0,0;	
GENF 202,'DYNAMIC1',.33,32,126,32,1,0,3,0,0,0;	
	GENerate Font dynamically
FONT 201;	Select the half-inch FONT just generated
MAP 5.25,2;	Move Absolute Position of cursor 5.25 inches right and 2 inches down the page
CTXT 'Super-Co 1st Quarter Notables';	print Centered TeXT string
FONT 202;	Select the one-third inch FONT just generated
MAP 2,3;	Move Absolute Position of cursor 2 inches right and 3 inches down
TEXT '* Revenue is up by 37%';	print TEXT string
MAP 2,4;	Move Absolute Position of cursor 2 inches right and 4 inches down
TEXT '* Net Profit has risen by 41%';	print TEXT string
MAP 2,5;	Move Absolute Position of cursor 2 inches right and 5 inches down
TEXT '* Employee count is up only 14%';	print TEXT string
EXIT;	EXIT the Prescribe sequence

```
!R!
RES;
SPO L;
GENF 201,'DYNAMIC1',.5,32,126,32,1,0,3,0,0,0;
GENF 202,'DYNAMIC1',.33,32,126,32,1,0,3,0,0,0;
FONT 201;
MAP 5.25,2;
CTXT 'Super-Co 1st Quarter Notables';
FONT 202;
MAP 2,3;
TEXT '*  Revenue is up by 37%';
MAP 2,4;
TEXT '*  Net Profit has risen by 41%';
MAP 2,5;
TEXT '*  Employee count is up only 14%';
EXIT;
```

Figure 6-7. Prescribe Sequence for creating a business presentation in WordStar. Use this sample as a guide for multiple-page presentations as well.

Unlike most of the other examples in this book, this one uses no embedded text for the word processing program. The text to be printed is all in Prescribe text commands. In some ways, control of the page is simpler using Prescribe commands because you're not trying to get two programs—the word processor and the Prescribe language—to work together.

In the sequence, the font-generating command (GENF) appears to be the most foreboding because of its string of numbers. Those numbers are options for the type of font you're generating. For instance, the first number (201) is simply the number of the font you're creating, and the .5 after the font name sets the height of the font. Each of the other numbers has a similar special meaning. To understand the GENF command and its options, refer to the *Prescribe Programmer's Reference Manual*.

Also notice that the horizontal coordinate of the MAP command is 5.25, not 5.5, which would evenly divide an 11-inch wide sheet of paper along its horizontal axis (in landscape mode). But 5.25 on each side of the center only adds up to 10.5 inches, and seemingly puts the cursor a half inch shy of the center. The reason to use 5.25 is due to the way the Kyocera aligns the

printer for the MAP command. The printer starts at the left margin of the print area, which is in 5 centimeters from the physical left edge of the paper. To compensate for that 5 cm, .25 inches is subtracted from the horizontal coordinate of the MAP command, to yield 5.25.

The CTXT command prints the headline text in the 201 font, centered at the location of the cursor. The next portion of the sequence selects the second generated font (202), and then repositions the cursor to print the text for the first bullet. Each TEXT command prints a line on the bullet chart.

By using this example you'll be able to print the title of each page in 1/2-inch text using FONT 201, and the bullet items in 1/3-inch text using FONT 202. Of course, you can make adjustments to the font sizes and line spacing for your own transparencies.

Super-Co 1st Quarter Notables

* Revenue is up by 37%

* Net Profit has risen by 41%

* Employee count is up only 14%

Figure 6-8. Business presentation printed in landscape orientation on transparency sheet for overhead projectors.

Brightening Up Your Presentation

Often, a business presentation can get boring, especially if the slides are all words with no graphic elements to add visual interest. To improve the look of your overheads, place a border around the entire page by using the BOX command. Use the examples in Chapter 10 of this book to see how to draw borders around the entire slide, or around portions of text on the slide. You use the Prescribe BOX command to draw the borders.

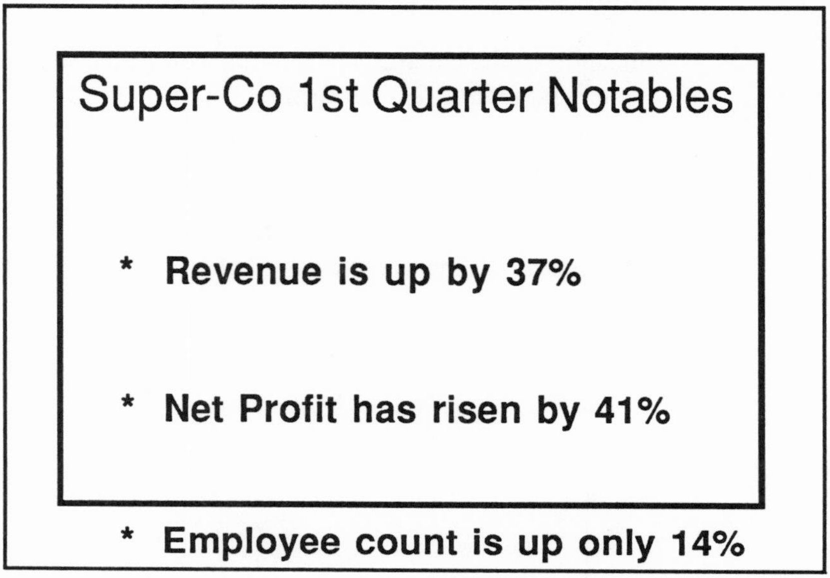

Figure 6-9. Spruce up your presentation with borders (see Chapter 10 for examples).

Before You Print

Because the text and formatting controls for the presentation pages are entirely in Prescribe commands, you don't have to make any changes in the word processing program prior to printing. The printing functions of the WordStar program won't alter the pages at all. Usually, the worst that can happen is an occasional blank page caused by the program repaginating pages of commands that are more than one page in length. Another benefit of using only Prescribe commands is that you don't have to be concerned with the type of printer driver program installed for the word processing program.

Multi-Page Considerations

Of course, business presentations are rarely one page long. In order to print multiple presentation pages, you add the PAGE command between the sequences for each page in your presentation. Then, for each page, repeat the commands that start with the first font selection right after the GENF commands.

So you don't have to retype all of the commands, use your word processing program's copy-and-paste function to copy the relevant commands, and insert them just prior to the EXIT command. Remember that the EXIT command must be the last command in the sequence. Using the copy-and-paste technique, you can create as many pages as you need, and then just edit the text for each page.

The benefit of duplicating the information page-by-page in this manner is two-fold: first, copying correct sequences avoids typographical errors; and second, you can be sure that the formats of subsequent slides are the same as the first one. Thus you can duplicate as many as you need and then edit the text for each new page, concentrating on the message content and not on the mechanics of getting it on the page.

In fact, as you develop more presentations with Prescribe, save the sequences you use to create the slides. You can then re-use those sequences for later presentations by editing the text in the TEXT commands. Eventually, you'll have a library of slide examples and corresponding sequences for creating captivating presentations.

HP LASERJET AND MICROSOFT WORD

Presentation transparencies are displayed with an overhead projector, often in a large room and to a large audience. Therefore, you'll want to use a large, crisp font that reads well from all corners of the room. Part of this example shows how to use other fonts to supplement the Laserjet's built-in fonts. Those built-in fonts are only intended for letters and other documents, not for overhead transparencies.

The fonts in this example are soft fonts that may be downloaded, or cartridge fonts that you can select. Both the downloading and font selection is done using PCL commands. If you don't have fonts large enough for transparencies, check with your Hewlett-Packard dealer or representative. Once you've selected a font, refer to Chapter 4 in this book for details about larger fonts.

Here is the sequence you'll use for a bullet chart. The bullet symbol is the asterisk (*). On the chart the title is centered in a larger font, and each bullet point is left-justified in somewhat smaller type.

Command	Explanation
E_CE	Reset printer options to default
E_C&l0O	Set Page Orientation to Landscape

Place the font selection commands here for the slide's title font. The specific commands depend on the font you choose for your LaserJet.

E_C*p1575X	Move Absolute Position of cursor 5.25 inches right
E_C*p600Y	Move Absolute Position of cursor 2 inches down

Next, enter the following line of text for the title of the slide:

Super-Co 1st Quarter Notables

Place the font selection commands here for the font you choose for the bullet text.

E_C*p600X	Move Absolute Position of cursor 2 inches right
E_C*p900Y	Move Absolute Position of cursor 3 inches down

Here is the text for the first bullet point:

* Revenue is up by 37%

E$_C$*p600X	Move Absolute Position of cursor 2 inches right
E$_C$*p1200Y	Move Absolute Position of cursor 4 inches down

Here is the text of the second bullet point:

* Net Profit has risen by 41%

E$_C$*p600X	Move Absolute Position of cursor 2 inches right
E$_C$*p1500Y	Move Absolute Position of cursor 5 inches down

And here is the third and final bullet point:

* Employee count is up only 14%

Like PCL cursor positioning commands in other examples in this book, the positions are calculated relative to 300 dots per inch. For example, a 2-inch movement is 600 dots.

The headline text will be centered on the page, and should be printed in a larger font, depending on which one you selected. On standard size pages, a 48-point font usually projects well. The font for the bullet text should be smaller, between 24 points and 36 points.

Note that you repeat the cursor positioning commands between each text line. These commands move the cursor down to the next text line and return the cursor to the left margin so each line begins left-justified. Of course, you can make adjustments to the font sizes and line spacing to suit your own tastes.

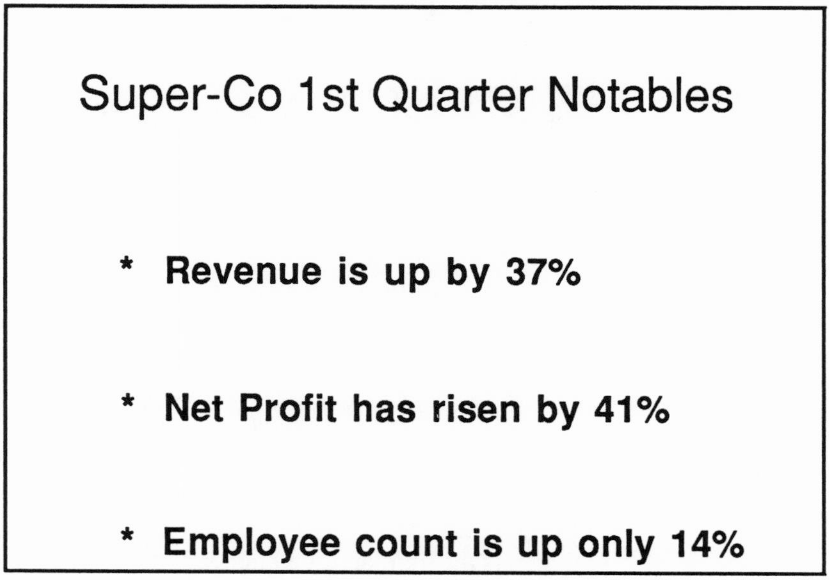

Super-Co 1st Quarter Notables

* **Revenue is up by 37%**

* **Net Profit has risen by 41%**

* **Employee count is up only 14%**

Figure 6-10. Business presentation printed in landscape orientation on transparency sheet for overhead projectors.

Often, a business presentation can get boring, especially if the slides are all words with no graphic elements to add visual interest. To improve the look of the overheads, you can use PCL commands to place a horizontal rule at the top and bottom of the slides. Use the examples in Chapter 8 to see how to draw rules above and below text.

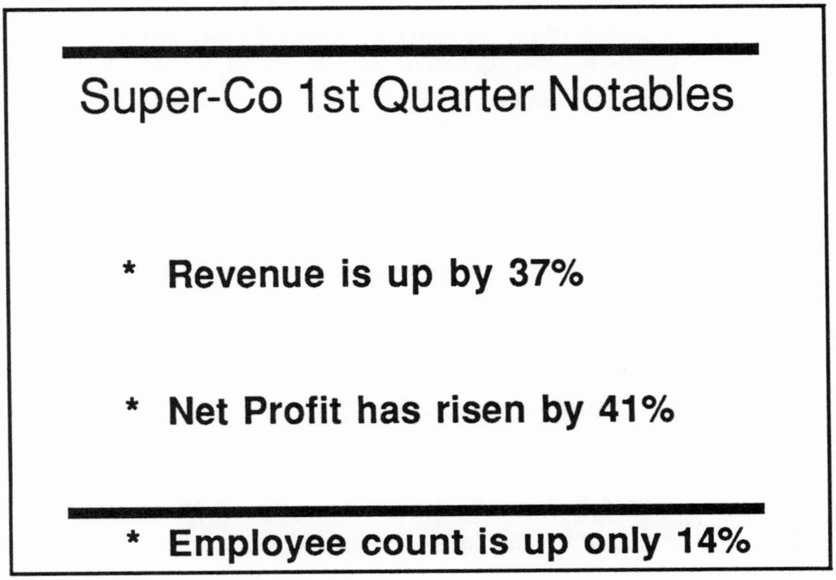

Figure 6-11. Spruce up your presentation with borders (see Chapter 8 for examples).

Before You Print

Probably the safest drivers to use for printing transparencies is TTY, DRAFT, or PLAIN. One or more of these drivers should be available in your word processing program. Some programs also have drivers specifically for the LaserJet, but you'll need to experiment with them to make sure that they transmit the Prescribe sequences to the printer correctly. If you have trouble getting the LaserJet to print slides similar to those shown in the examples, change your selection of a printer driver to one of the ones listed above. Usually the worst problem that occurs when using one of these drivers is an occasional blank page that results when the word processing program repaginates sequences of commands that are more than one page long.

Multi-Page Considerations

Of course, business presentations are rarely one page long. In order to make multiple presentation pages, simply add a page break using the page break command in WORD. Then, to create another page for a transparency, repeat the commands starting with the first font selection right after the page orientation command.

So you don't have to retype all of the commands, use your word processing program's copy-and-paste function to copy the relevant commands. Using the copy-and-paste technique, you can create as many pages as you need, and then just edit the text for each page.

The benefit of duplicating the information page-by-page in this manner is two-fold: first, copying correct sequences avoids typographical errors; and second, you can be sure that the formats of subsequent slides are the same as the first one. Thus you can duplicate as many as you need and then edit the text for each new page, concentrating on the message content and not on the mechanics of getting it on the page.

In fact, as you develop more presentations with PCL, save the sequences you use to create the slides. You can then re-use those sequences for later presentations by editing the text. Eventually, you'll have a library of slide examples and corresponding sequences for creating captivating presentations.

HP LASERJET AND MULTIMATE

Presentation transparencies are displayed with an overhead projector, often in a large room and to a large audience. Therefore, you'll want to use a large, crisp font that reads well from all corners of the room. Part of this example shows how to use other fonts to supplement the Laserjet's built-in fonts. Those built-in fonts are only intended for letters and other documents, not for overhead transparencies.

The fonts in this example are soft fonts that may be downloaded, or cartridge fonts that you can select. Both the downloading and font selection is done using PCL commands. If you don't have fonts large enough for transparencies, check with your Hewlett-Packard dealer or representative. Once you've selected a font, refer to Chapter 4 in this book for details about larger fonts.

Here is the sequence you'll use for a bullet chart. The bullet symbol is the asterisk (*). On the chart the title is centered in a larger font, and each bullet point is left-justified in somewhat smaller type.

Command	Explanation
E_CE	Reset printer options to default
E_C&l0O	Set Page Orientation to Landscape

Place the font selection commands here for the slide's title font. The specific commands depend on the font you choose for your LaserJet.

E_C*p1575X	Move Absolute Position of cursor 5.25 inches right
E_C*p600Y	Move Absolute Position of cursor 2 inches down

Next, enter the following line of text for the title of the slide:

Super-Co 1st Quarter Notables

Place the font selection commands here for the font you choose for the bullet text.

E_C*p600X	Move Absolute Position of cursor 2 inches right
E_C*p900Y	Move Absolute Position of cursor 3 inches down

Here is the text for the first bullet point:

* Revenue is up by 37%
E_C*p600X   Move Absolute Position of cursor 2 inches
                              right
E_C*p1200Y   Move Absolute Position of cursor 4 inches
                              down

Here is the text of the second bullet point:

* Net Profit has risen by 41%
E_C*p600X   Move Absolute Position of cursor 2 inches
                              right
E_C*p1500Y   Move Absolute Position of cursor 5 inches
                              down

And here is the third and final bullet point:

* Employee count is up only 14%

Like PCL cursor positioning commands in other examples in this book, the positions are calculated relative to 300 dots per inch. For example, a 2-inch movement is 600 dots.

The headline text will be centered on the page, and should be printed in a larger font, depending on which one you selected. On standard size pages, a 48-point font usually projects well. The font for the bullet text should be smaller, between 24 points and 36 points.

Note that you repeat the cursor positioning commands between each text line. These commands move the cursor down to the next text line and return the cursor to the left margin so each line begins left-justified. Of course, you can make adjustments to the font sizes and line spacing to suit your own tastes.

Super-Co 1st Quarter Notables

* **Revenue is up by 37%**

* **Net Profit has risen by 41%**

* **Employee count is up only 14%**

Figure 6-12. Business presentation printed in landscape orientation on transparency sheet for overhead projectors.

Often, a business presentation can get boring, especially if the slides are all words with no graphic elements to add visual interest. To improve the look of the overheads, you can use PCL commands to place a horizontal rule at the top and bottom of the slides. Use the examples in Chapter 8 to see how to draw rules above and below text.

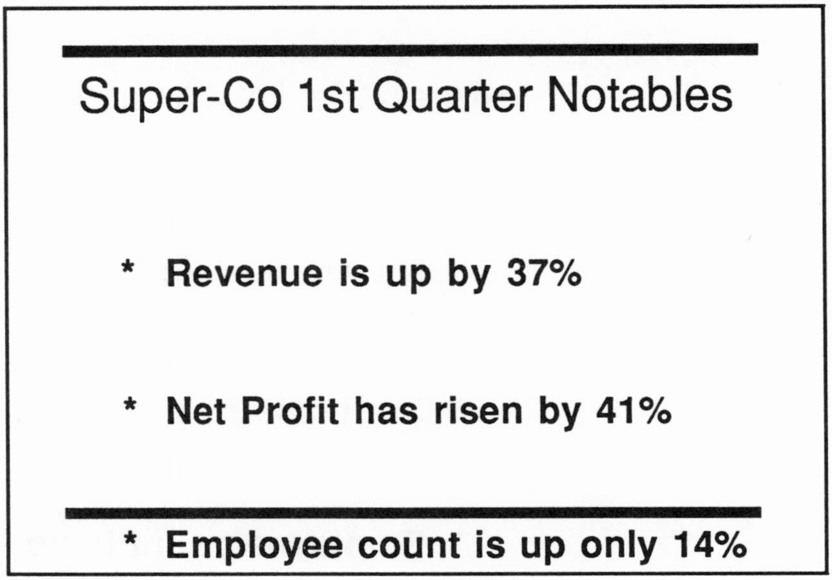

Figure 6-13. Spruce up your presentation with borders (see Chapter 8 for examples).

Before You Print

Probably the safest drivers to use for printing transparencies is TTY, DRAFT or PLAIN. One or more of these drivers should be available in your word processing program. Some programs also have drivers specifically for the LaserJet, but you'll need to experiment with them to make sure that they transmit the Prescribe sequences to the printer correctly. If you have trouble getting the LaserJet to print slides similar to those shown in the examples, change your selection of a printer driver to one of the ones listed above. Usually the worst problem that occurs when using one of these drivers is an occasional blank page that results when the word processing program repaginates sequences of commands that are more than one page long.

Multi-Page Considerations

Of course, business presentations are rarely one page long. In order to make multiple presentation pages, simply add a page break using the page break command in MultiMate. Then, to create another page for a transparency, repeat the commands starting with the first font selection right after the page orientation command.

So you don't have to retype all of the commands, use your word processing program's copy-and-paste function to copy the relevant commands. Using the copy-and-paste technique, you can create as many pages as you need, and then just edit the text for each page.

The benefit of duplicating the information page-by-page in this manner is two-fold: first, copying correct sequences avoids typographical errors; and second, you can be sure that the formats of subsequent slides are the same as the first one. Thus you can duplicate as many as you need and then edit the text for each new page, concentrating on the message content and not on the mechanics of getting it on the page.

In fact, as you develop more presentations with PCL, save the sequences you use to create the slides. You can then re-use those sequences for later presentations by editing the text. Eventually, you'll have a library of slide examples and corresponding sequences for creating captivating presentations.

HP LASERJET AND WORDSTAR

Presentation transparencies are displayed with an overhead projector, often in a large room and to a large audience. Therefore, you'll want to use a large, crisp font that reads well from all corners of the room. Part of this example shows how to use other fonts to supplement the Laserjet's built-in fonts. Those built-in fonts are only intended for letters and other documents, not for overhead transparencies.

The fonts in this example are soft fonts that may be downloaded, or cartridge fonts that you can select. Both the downloading and font selection is done using PCL commands. If you don't have fonts large enough for transparencies, check with your Hewlett-Packard dealer or representative. Once you've selected a font, refer to Chapter 4 in this book for details about larger fonts.

Here is the sequence you'll use for a bullet chart. The bullet symbol is the asterisk (*). On the chart the title is centered in a larger font, and each bullet point is left-justified in somewhat smaller type.

<u>Command</u>	<u>Explanation</u>
E_CE	Reset printer options to default
E_C&l0O	Set Page Orientation to Landscape

Place the font selection commands here for the slide's title font. The specific commands depend on the font you choose for your LaserJet.

E_C*p1575X	Move Absolute Position of cursor 5.25 inches right
E_C*p600Y	Move Absolute Position of cursor 2 inches down

Next, enter the following line of text for the title of the slide:

Super-Co 1st Quarter Notables

Place the font selection commands here for the font you choose for the bullet text.

E_C*p600X	Move Absolute Position of cursor 2 inches right
E_C*p900Y	Move Absolute Position of cursor 3 inches down

Here is the text for the first bullet point:

```
* Revenue is up by 37%
```
E_C*p600X   Move Absolute Position of cursor 2 inches right

E_C*p1200Y   Move Absolute Position of cursor 4 inches down

Here is the text of the second bullet point:

```
* Net Profit has risen by 41%
```
E_C*p600X   Move Absolute Position of cursor 2 inches right

E_C*p1500Y   Move Absolute Position of cursor 5 inches down

And here is the third and final bullet point:

```
* Employee count is up only 14%
```

Like PCL cursor positioning commands in other examples in this book, the positions are calculated relative to 300 dots per inch. For example, a 2-inch movement is 600 dots.

The headline text will be centered on the page, and should be printed in a larger font, depending on which one you selected. On standard size pages, a 48-point font usually projects well. The font for the bullet text should be smaller, between 24 points and 36 points.

Note that you repeat the cursor positioning commands between each text line. These commands move the cursor down to the next text line and return the cursor to the left margin so each line begins left-justified. Of course, you can make adjustments to the font sizes and line spacing to suit your own tastes.

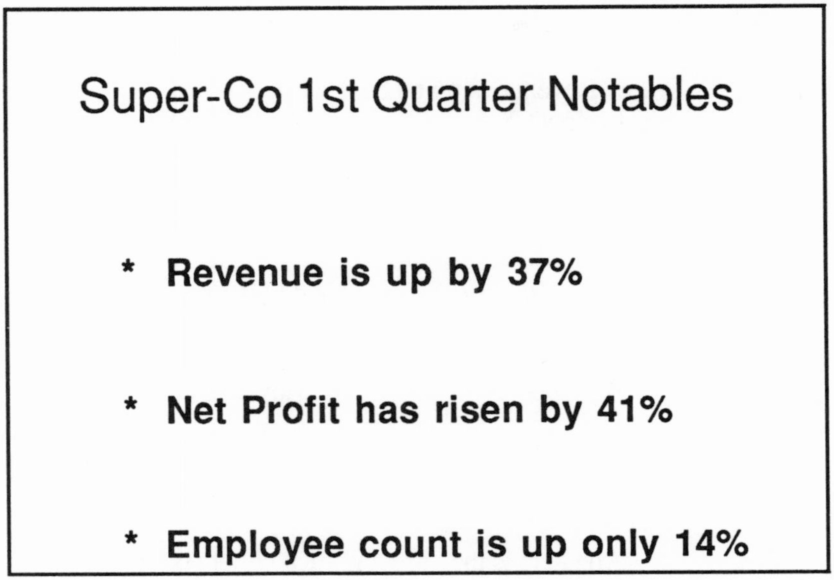

Super-Co 1st Quarter Notables

* **Revenue is up by 37%**

* **Net Profit has risen by 41%**

* **Employee count is up only 14%**

Figure 6-14. Business presentation printed in landscape orientation on transparency sheet for overhead projectors.

Often, a business presentation can get boring, especially if the slides are all words with no graphic elements to add visual interest. To improve the look of the overheads, you can use PCL commands to place a horizontal rule at the top and bottom of the slides. Use the examples in Chapter 8 to see how to draw rules above and below text.

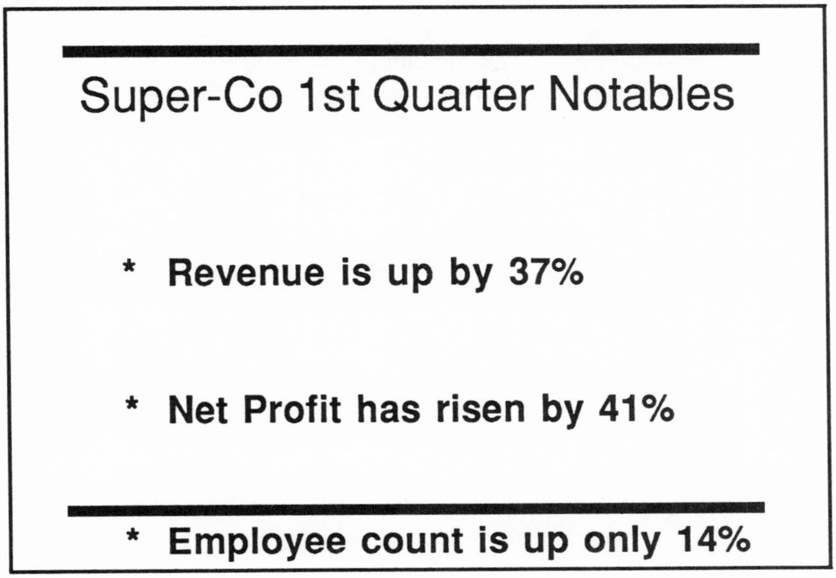

Figure 6-15. Spruce up your presentation with borders (see Chapter 8 for examples).

Before You Print

Probably the safest drivers to use for printing transparencies is TTY, DRAFT, or PLAIN. One or more of these drivers should be available in your word processing program. Some programs also have drivers specifically for the LaserJet, but you'll need to experiment with them to make sure that they transmit the Prescribe sequences to the printer correctly. If you have trouble getting the LaserJet to print slides similar to those shown in the examples, change your selection of a printer driver to one of the ones listed above. Usually the worst problem that occurs when using one of these drivers is an occasional blank page that results when the word processing program repaginates sequences of commands that are more than one page long.

Multi-Page Considerations

Of course, business presentations are rarely one page long. In order to make multiple presentation pages, simply add a page break using the page break command in WordStar. Then, to create another page for a transparency, repeat the commands starting with the first font selection right after the page orientation command.

So you don't have to retype all of the commands, use your word processing program's copy-and-paste function to copy the relevant commands. Using the copy-and-paste technique, you can create as many pages as you need, and then just edit the text for each page.

The benefit of duplicating the information page-by-page in this manner is two-fold: first, copying correct sequences avoids typographical errors; and second, you can be sure that the formats of subsequent slides are the same as the first one. Thus you can duplicate as many as you need and then edit the text for each new page, concentrating on the message content and not on the mechanics of getting it on the page.

In fact, as you develop more presentations with PCL, save the sequences you use to create the slides. You can then re-use those sequences for later presentations by editing the text. Eventually, you'll have a library of slide examples and corresponding sequences for creating captivating presentations.

Chapter 7

Printing a Pleading Document

A pleading document is a special format for legal text. A pleading document numbers each line of text with numbers running vertically down the left margin. In addition, vertical ruled lines in both margins bracket the text. If you work in a law firm or produce legal documents in your daily work, this application will let you print pleading documents using commands from your word processing program.

KYOCERA AND MICROSOFT WORD

In this example you'll create a Prescribe macro for printing the pleading document. After writing the macro, you'll save it in a file for future use. You'll also see how to download the macro to the Kyocera, and then call it for printing pleading documents from Microsoft WORD.

Creating the Macro for a Pleading Document

The macro to print the pleading document contains the commands for printing line numbers and vertical lines down the side of each page. Here's the Prescribe sequence for the macro:

Command	Explanation
!R!	staRt Prescribe sequence
DELM PLEAD;	DELete Macro named PLEAD
MCRO PLEAD;	create new MaCRO named PLEAD
SCF;	Save Current Font selection
SCP;	Save Current Position of cursor
FTMD 13;	set attributes of FonT MoDe
UNIT D;	set UNIT of measure to Dots (300 per inch)
SPD 1;	Set Pen Diameter to 1 dot (1/300 inch)
UNIT I;	set UNIT of measure to Inches
MZP1.082,0;	Move to Zero-relative Position to draw first vertical rule in left margin
DRP 0,11;	Draw to Relative Position first vertical rule
MZP1.051,0;	Move to Zero-relative Position to draw second vertical rule in left margin
DRP 0,11;	Draw to Relative Position second vertical rule
MZP 8.028,0;	Move to Zero-relative Position to draw vertical rule in right margin
DRP 0,11;	Draw to Relative Position vertical rule on right
SLPI 3;	Set Lines Per Inch to three
FONT 1;	select FONT Courier Portrait 12 point
MZP 0.905,1.440;	Move to Zero-relative Position for numbering
MRP 0,%1;	Move Relative Position down as specified in the macro call to start first line number
TEXT '1',L;	print TEXT (number 1) and advance one Line
MRP -0.01,0;	Move Relative Position left to compensate for the narrow number 1.

TEXT '2',L;	print TEXT (line 2) and advance one Line
TEXT '3',L;	
TEXT '4',L;	
TEXT '5',L;	
TEXT '6',L;	
TEXT '7',L;	
TEXT '8',L;	
TEXT '9',L;	
MRP -0.098,0;	Move Relative Position left for two digit numbers
TEXT '10',L;	print TEXT (the line number) and advance one Line
TEXT '11',L;	
TEXT '12',L;	
TEXT '13',L;	
TEXT '14',L;	
TEXT '15',L;	
TEXT '16',L;	
TEXT '17',L;	
TEXT '18',L;	
TEXT '19',L;	
TEXT '20',L;	
TEXT '21',L;	
TEXT '22',L;	
TEXT '23',L;	
TEXT '24',L;	
TEXT '25',L;	
TEXT '26',L;	
RPP;	Restore Previous Position of cursor
RPF;	Restore Previous Font selection
SLPI 6;	Set Lines Per Inch to six
ENDM;	END the Macro definition
EXIT;	EXIT Prescribe sequence

Enter this series of Prescribe commands as a new document, and save it as an ASCII file using the Unformatted option. Give the file an appropriate name such as PLEAD.MAC. For more details on creating macros, refer to the examples in Chapter 5 of this book, and to the instructions in the *Kyocera Programming Manual*.

Commands to note include the DELM command which deletes any earlier macro named PLEAD. This assures that any macro already entered for testing gets deleted before you try again.

The first MRP command drops the cursor vertically the number of inches you specify when you call the PLEAD macro at the top of each page in your document. If you don't need to vary the starting position of the number, eliminate this command from the macro. Also eliminate the number parameter in the CALL command of the calling sequence shown below.

The double and single vertical rules in the left and right margin of the pleading document, respectively, are printed by the MZP and DRP command pairs right after the UNIT I command.

The series of TEXT commands prints line numbers from one to 26. In preparation for the line numbers, the SLPI command sets the printer to three lines per inch. After the line numbers are printed the laser is set back to six lines per inch, and you must use double spacing in the text of the document. Notice the slight adjustment in the horizontal cursor positioning to make the different-sized numbers line up properly.

An alternate method of vertically aligning the numbers would be to set the right margin at the right side of the numbers (about one inch from the left margin) temporarily by using the SRM command. Then, print each line number with the RTXT command which prints text in right-justified mode. Be sure to set the right margin back to its normal position after the line numbering is done.

Downloading the Pleading Macro

To use the pleading macro, you must first download it from the PC to the Kyocera printer. To accomplish this from DOS, enter the command COPY PLEAD.MAC PRN. This command copies the PLEAD.MAC file to the printer. Each time you turn the printer on, you have to enter this DOS command.

To automate the process of downloading the macro, put the DOS command in your AUTOEXEC.BAT file. Then, each time your PC is turned on the macro for your pleading document will be automatically downloaded, ready to use.

Now that the macro has been downloaded to the printer, you can call the macro by placing a calling sequence at the top of each page to be printed. The pages will have their lines numbered and will have the required vertical lines in the proper places.

Calling the Pleading Macro

Enter the following Prescribe commands at the top of each page that you want numbered and lined as a pleading document:

Command   Explanation

!R!   staRt Prescribe sequence
CALL PLEAD,1.5;   CALL macro PLEAD, start line numbers at 1.5
                           inches down the page
EXIT,E;   EXIT Prescribe sequence — ignore carriage
                           return

```
!R!CALL PLEAD,1.5;EXIT,E;
          In CONGRESS, July 4, 1776.

     The unanimous Declaration of the

     thirteen united States of America,

  When in the course of human events it becomes

necessary for one people to dissolve the political

bands which have connected them with another, and

to assume among the powers of the earth, the

separate and equal station to which the Laws of
```

Figure 7-1. Prescribe sequence at the top of the Declaration of Independence.

When you include this macro at the top of your legal documents, they will print with line numbers down the left margin and ruled lines in both margins. You may have to specify how far down the page to position the first line number in order to align the numbers with each line of text. For example, you may want to have the numbers start lower on the first page, and higher on the second and remaining pages. Experiment with the number parameter at

the end of the CALL command in the sequence to coordinate it with the margin settings for the top of the page.

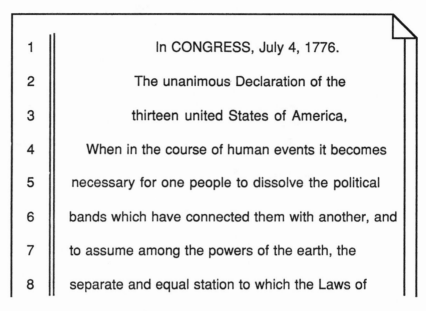

1   In CONGRESS, July 4, 1776.

2   The unanimous Declaration of the

3   thirteen united States of America,

4   When in the course of human events it becomes

5   necessary for one people to dissolve the political

6   bands which have connected them with another, and

7   to assume among the powers of the earth, the

8   separate and equal station to which the Laws of

Figure 7-2. Declaration of Independence on a pleading document.

Before You Print

Here are some guidelines for getting the pleading document to print correctly.

First, set your printer to use the KCF3010P driver.

When entering the Prescribe sequence to call the pleading macro, enter it on one line, like this: !R!;CALL PLEAD,1.5;EXIT,E;. Then, enter a carriage return and start typing the text of the document. By using the E parameter with the EXIT command, you tell the Kyocera to ignore the carriage return immediately following the command sequence. If you forget the E parameter on the EXIT command, your text will all be one line below the numbers.

For best results, set the line spacing at two lines per inch., then set your margins as follows:

Left	1.25 inches
Top	1.7 inches
Bottom	.8 inches
Right	.5 inches

Once the macro for the pleading document is complete, place the DOS downloading command in your AUTOEXEC.BAT file. The macro will then be downloaded to the printer each time you start the computer and will make using the macro as simple as choosing a command from your word processing program. In short, you'll be able to print pleading documents without much effort at all.

KYOCERA AND MULTIMATE

In this example you'll create a Prescribe macro for printing the pleading document. After writing the macro, you'll save it in a file for future use. You'll also see how to download the macro to the Kyocera, and then call it for printing pleading documents from MultiMate.

Creating the Macro for a Pleading Document

The macro to print the pleading document contains the commands for printing line numbers and vertical lines down the side of each page. Here's the Prescribe sequence for the macro:

Command	Explanation
!R!	staRt Prescribe sequence
DELM PLEAD;	DELete Macro named PLEAD
MCRO PLEAD;	create new MaCRO named PLEAD
SCF;	Save Current Font selection
SCP;	Save Current Position of cursor
FTMD 13;	set attributes of FonT MoDe
UNIT D;	set UNIT of measure to Dots (300 per inch)
SPD 1;	Set Pen Diameter to 1 dot (1/300 inch)
UNIT I;	set UNIT of measure to Inches
MZP1.082,0;	Move to Zero-relative Position to draw first vertical rule in left margin
DRP 0,11;	Draw to Relative Position first vertical rule
MZP1.051,0;	Move to Zero-relative Position to draw second vertical rule in left margin
DRP 0,11;	Draw to Relative Position second vertical rule
MZP 8.028,0;	Move to Zero-relative Position to draw vertical rule in right margin
DRP 0,11;	Draw to Relative Position vertical rule on right
SLPI 3;	Set Lines Per Inch to three
FONT 1;	select FONT Courier Portrait 12 point
MZP 0.905,1.440;	Move to Zero-relative Position for numbering
MRP 0,%1;	Move Relative Position down as specified in the macro call to start first line number
TEXT '1',L;	print TEXT (number 1) and advance one Line

MRP -0.01,0;	Move Relative Position left to compensate for the narrow number 1.
TEXT '2',L;	print TEXT (line 2) and advance one Line
TEXT '3',L;	
TEXT '4',L;	
TEXT '5',L;	
TEXT '6',L;	
TEXT '7',L;	
TEXT '8',L;	
TEXT '9',L;	
MRP -0.098,0;	Move Relative Position left for two digit numbers
TEXT '10',L;	print TEXT (the line number) and advance one Line
TEXT '11',L;	
TEXT '12',L;	
TEXT '13',L;	
TEXT '14',L;	
TEXT '15',L;	
TEXT '16',L;	
TEXT '17',L;	
TEXT '18',L;	
TEXT '19',L;	
TEXT '20',L;	
TEXT '21',L;	
TEXT '22',L;	
TEXT '23',L;	
TEXT '24',L;	
TEXT '25',L;	
TEXT '26',L;	
RPP;	Restore Previous Position of cursor
RPF;	Restore Previous Font selection
SLPI 6;	Set Lines Per Inch to six
ENDM;	END the Macro definition
EXIT;	EXIT Prescribe sequence

Enter this series of Prescribe commands as a new document, and save it as an ASCII file using the Unformatted option. Give the file an appropriate name such as PLEAD.MAC. For more details on creating macros, refer to the examples in Chapter 5 of this book, and to the instructions in the Kyocera Programming Manual.

Commands to note include the DELM command which deletes any earlier macro named PLEAD. This assures that any macro you already entered for testing gets deleted before you try again.

The first MRP command drops the cursor vertically the number of inches you specify when you call the PLEAD macro at the top of each page in your document. If you don't need to vary the starting position of the number, eliminate this command from the macro. Also eliminate the number parameter in the CALL command of the calling sequence shown below.

The double and single vertical rules in the left and right margin of the pleading document, respectively, are printed by the MZP and DRP command pairs right after the UNIT I command.

The series of TEXT commands prints line numbers from one to 26. In preparation for the line numbers, the SLPI command sets the printer to three lines per inch. After the line numbers are printed the laser is set back to six lines per inch, and you must use double spacing in the text of the document. Notice the slight adjustment in the horizontal cursor positioning to make the different-sized numbers line up properly.

An alternate method of vertically aligning the numbers would be to set the right margin at the right side of the numbers (about one inch from the left margin) temporarily by using the SRM command. Then, print each line number with the RTXT command which prints text in right-justified mode. Be sure to set the right margin back to its normal position after the line numbering is done.

Downloading the Pleading Macro

To use the pleading macro, you must first download it from the PC to the Kyocera printer. To accomplish this from DOS, enter the command COPY PLEAD.MAC PRN. This command copies the PLEAD.MAC file to the printer. Each time you turn the printer on, you have to enter this DOS command.

To automate the process of downloading the macro, put the DOS command in your AUTOEXEC.BAT file. Then, each time your PC is turned on the macro for your pleading document will be automatically downloaded, ready to use.

Now that the macro has been downloaded to the printer, you can call the macro by placing a calling sequence at the top of each page to be printed. The pages will have their lines numbered and will have the required vertical lines in the proper places.

Calling the Pleading Macro

Enter the following Prescribe commands at the top of each page that you want numbered and lined as a pleading document:

Command	Explanation
!R!	staRt Prescribe sequence
CALL PLEAD,1.5;	CALL macro PLEAD, start line numbers at 1.5 inches down the page
EXIT,E;	EXIT Prescribe sequence — ignore carriage return

```
!R!CALL PLEAD,1.5;EXIT,E;
            In CONGRESS, July 4, 1776.

     The unanimous Declaration of the

     thirteen united States of America,

   When in the course of human events it becomes

necessary for one people to dissolve the political

bands which have connected them with another, and

to assume among the powers of the earth, the

separate and equal station to which the Laws of
```

Figure 7-3. Prescribe sequence at the top of the Declaration of Independence.

When you include this macro at the top of your legal documents, they will print with line numbers down the left margin and ruled lines in both margins. You may have to specify how far down the page to position the first line number in order to align the numbers with each line of text. For example, you may want to have the numbers start lower on the first page, and higher on the second and remaining pages. Experiment with the number parameter at

the end of the CALL command in the sequence to coordinate it with the margin settings for the top of the page.

1	In CONGRESS, July 4, 1776.
2	The unanimous Declaration of the
3	thirteen united States of America,
4	When in the course of human events it becomes
5	necessary for one people to dissolve the political
6	bands which have connected them with another, and
7	to assume among the powers of the earth, the
8	separate and equal station to which the Laws of

Figure 7-4. Declaration of Independence on a pleading document.

Before You Print

Here are some guidelines for getting the pleading document to print correctly.

Set your printer to use the KYOPOR driver.

When entering the Prescribe sequence to call the pleading macro, enter it on one line, like this: !R!;CALL PLEAD,1.5;EXIT,E;. Then, enter a carriage return and start typing the text of the document. By using the E parameter with the EXIT command, you tell the Kyocera to ignore the carriage return immediately following the command sequence. If you forget the E parameter on the EXIT command, your text will all be one line below the numbers.

For best results, MultiMate's Print Format Menu should specify the following:

Default Pitch	1
Left Margin	12
Top Margin	7
Double Space	Yes (You can also specify this on the format line)
Pat	LJPLEAD

The right margin should be specified on the "Format Line" above the text, by moving the cursor to the position you want as the end of the line, such as column 67.

Once the macro for the pleading document is complete, place the DOS downloading command in your AUTOEXEC.BAT file. The macro will then be downloaded to the printer each time you start the computer and will make using the macro as simple as choosing a command from your word processing program. In short, you'll be able to print pleading documents without much effort at all.

KYOCERA AND WORDSTAR

In this example you'll create a Prescribe macro for printing the pleading document. After writing the macro, you'll save it in a file.for future use. You'll also see how to download the macro to the Kyocera, and then call it for printing pleading documents from WordStar.

Creating the Macro for a Pleading Document

The macro to print the pleading document contains the commands for printing line numbers and vertical lines down the side of each page. Here's the Prescribe sequence for the macro:

Command	Explanation
!R!	staRt Prescribe sequence
DELM PLEAD;	DELete Macro named PLEAD
MCRO PLEAD;	create new MaCRO named PLEAD
SCF;	Save Current Font selection
SCP;	Save Current Position of cursor
FTMD 13;	set attributes of FonT MoDe
UNIT D;	set UNIT of measure to Dots (300 per inch)
SPD 1;	Set Pen Diameter to 1 dot (1/300 inch)
UNIT I;	set UNIT of measure to Inches
MZP1.082,0;	Move to Zero-relative Position to draw first vertical rule in left margin
DRP 0,11;	Draw to Relative Position first vertical rule
MZP1.051,0;	Move to Zero-relative Position to draw second vertical rule in left margin
DRP 0,11;	Draw to Relative Position second vertical rule
MZP 8.028,0;	Move to Zero-relative Position to draw vertical rule in right margin
DRP 0,11;	Draw to Relative Position vertical rule on right
SLPI 3;	Set Lines Per Inch to three
FONT 1;	select FONT Courier Portrait 12 point
MZP 0.905,1.440;	Move to Zero-relative Position for numbering
MRP 0,%1;	Move Relative Position down as specified in the macro call to start first line number
TEXT '1',L;	print TEXT (number 1) and advance one Line

MRP -0.01,0;	Move Relative Position left to compensate for the narrow number 1.
TEXT '2',L;	print TEXT (line 2) and advance one Line
TEXT '3',L;	
TEXT '4',L;	
TEXT '5',L;	
TEXT '6',L;	
TEXT '7',L;	
TEXT '8',L;	
TEXT '9',L;	
MRP -0.098,0;	Move Relative Position left for two digit numbers
TEXT '10',L;	print TEXT (the line number) and advance one Line
TEXT '11',L;	
TEXT '12',L;	
TEXT '13',L;	
TEXT '14',L;	
TEXT '15',L;	
TEXT '16',L;	
TEXT '17',L;	
TEXT '18',L;	
TEXT '19',L;	
TEXT '20',L;	
TEXT '21',L;	
TEXT '22',L;	
TEXT '23',L;	
TEXT '24',L;	
TEXT '25',L;	
TEXT '26',L;	
RPP;	Restore Previous Position of cursor
RPF;	Restore Previous Font selection
SLPI 6;	Set Lines Per Inch to six
ENDM;	END the Macro definition
EXIT;	EXIT Prescribe sequence

Enter this series of Prescribe commands as a new document, and save it as an ASCII file using the Unformatted option. Give the file an appropriate name such as PLEAD.MAC. For more details on creating macros, refer to the examples in Chapter 5 of this book, and to the instructions in the *Kyocera Programming Manual*.

Commands to note include the DELM command which deletes any earlier macro named PLEAD. This assures that any macro you already entered for testing gets deleted before you try again.

The first MRP command drops the cursor vertically the number of inches you specify when you call the PLEAD macro at the top of each page in your document. If you don't need to vary the starting position of the number, eliminate this command from the macro. Also eliminate the number parameter in the CALL command of the calling sequence shown below.

The double and single vertical rules in the left and right margin of the pleading document, respectively, are printed by the MZP and DRP command pairs right after the UNIT I command.

The series of TEXT commands prints line numbers from one to 26. In preparation for the line numbers, the SLPI command sets the printer to three lines per inch. After the line numbers are printed the laser is set back to six lines per inch, and you must use double spacing in the text of the document. Notice the slight adjustment in the horizontal cursor positioning to make the different-sized numbers line up properly.

An alternate method of vertically aligning the numbers would be to set the right margin at the right side of the numbers (about one inch from the left margin) temporarily by using the SRM command. Then, print each line number with the RTXT command which prints text in right-justified mode. Be sure to set the right margin back to its normal position after the line numbering is done.

Downloading the Pleading Macro

To use the pleading macro, you must first download it from the PC to the Kyocera printer. To accomplish this from DOS, enter the command COPY PLEAD.MAC PRN. This command copies the PLEAD.MAC file to the printer. Each time you turn the printer on, you have to enter this DOS command.

To automate the process of downloading the macro, put the DOS command in your AUTOEXEC.BAT file. Then, each time your PC is turned on the macro for your pleading document will be automatically downloaded, ready to use.

Now that the macro has been downloaded to the printer, you can call the macro by placing a calling sequence at the top of each page to be printed. The pages will have their lines numbered and will have the required vertical lines in the proper places.

Calling the Pleading Macro

Enter the following Prescribe commands at the top of each page that you want numbered and lined as a pleading document:

Command	Explanation
!R!	staRt Prescribe sequence
CALL PLEAD,1.5;	CALL macro PLEAD, start line numbers at 1.5 inches down the page
EXIT,E;	EXIT Prescribe sequence — ignore carriage return

```
!R!CALL PLEAD,1.5;EXIT,E;
            In CONGRESS, July 4, 1776.

     The unanimous Declaration of the

       thirteen united States of America,

    When in the course of human events it becomes

necessary for one people to dissolve the political

bands which have connected them with another, and

to assume among the powers of the earth, the

separate and equal station to which the Laws of
```

Figure 7-5. Prescribe sequence at the top of the Declaration of Independence.

When you include this macro at the top of your legal documents, they will print with line numbers down the left margin and ruled lines in both margins. You may have to specify how far down the page to position the first line number in order to align the numbers with each line of text. For example, you may want to have the numbers start lower on the first page, and higher on the second and remaining pages. Experiment with the number parameter at

the end of the CALL command in the sequence to coordinate it with the margin settings for the top of the page.

1	In CONGRESS, July 4, 1776.
2	The unanimous Declaration of the
3	thirteen united States of America,
4	When in the course of human events it becomes
5	necessary for one people to dissolve the political
6	bands which have connected them with another, and
7	to assume among the powers of the earth, the
8	separate and equal station to which the Laws of

Figure 7-6. Declaration of Independence on a pleading document.

Before You Print

Here are some guidelines for getting the pleading document to print correctly.

When entering the Prescribe sequence to call the pleading macro, enter it on one line, like this: !R!;CALL PLEAD,1.5;EXIT,E;. Then, enter a carriage return and start typing the text of the document. By using the E parameter with the EXIT command, you tell the Kyocera to ignore the carriage return immediately following the command sequence. If you forget the E parameter on the EXIT command, your text will all be one line below the numbers.

For best results, use the .LS2 command for double spacing, and the .PA command wherever you want a page break. You should use a Control-B in each paragraph when you want to change the formatting. When printing your document, use Form Feeds = YES and DRAFT printer.

Once the macro for the pleading document is complete, place the DOS downloading command in your AUTOEXEC.BAT file. The macro will then be downloaded to the printer each time you start the computer and will make using the macro as simple as choosing a command from your word processing program. In short, you'll be able to print pleading documents without much effort at all.

HP LASERJET AND MICROSOFT WORD

In this example you'll create a PCL macro for printing the pleading document. After writing the macro, you'll save it in a file for future use. You'll also see how to download the macro to the LaserJet, and then call it for printing pleading documents from WORD.

Creating the Macro for a Pleading Document

The macro to print the pleading document contains the commands for printing line numbers and vertical lines down the side of each page. Here's the PCL sequence for the macro:

Command	Explanation
E_C&f8y0X	Establish a Macro ID and start the
E_C&a10C‖E_C&a+68C‖	Macro definition. Move the horizontal
E_C&a10C‖E_C&a+68C‖	cursor to column 10 and print the
E_C&a10C‖E_C&a+68C‖	double vertical line. Then move to
E_C&a10C‖E_C&a+68C‖	column 68 and print the single vertical
E_C&a10C‖E_C&a+68C‖	line. The carriage returns at the end of
	each command pair takes care of
	vertical cursor positioning.
E_C&a9C1E_C&a10C‖E_C&a+68C‖	Move the horizontal cursor to column
E_C&a10C‖E_C&a+68C‖	9 and print the line number.
E_C&a9C2E_C&a10C‖E_C&a+68C‖	Repeat the double and single
E_C&a10C‖E_C&a+68C‖	verticalline commands.
E_C&a9C3E_C&a10C‖E_C&a+68C‖	This command sequence
E_C&a10C‖E_C&a+68C‖	repeats through line 26.
E_C&a9C4E_C&a10C‖E_C&a+68C‖	
E_C&a10C‖E_C&a+68C‖	
E_C&a9C5E_C&a10C‖E_C&a+68C‖	
E_C&a10C‖E_C&a+68C‖	
E_C&a9C6E_C&a10C‖E_C&a+68C‖	
E_C&a10C‖E_C&a+68C‖	
E_C&a9C7E_C&a10C‖E_C&a+68C‖	
E_C&a10C‖E_C&a+68C‖	
E_C&a9C8E_C&a10C‖E_C&a+68C‖	
E_C&a10C‖E_C&a+68C‖	
E_C&a9C9E_C&a10C‖E_C&a+68C‖	
E_C&a10C‖E_C&a+68C‖	
E_C&a8C10E_C&a10C‖E_C&a+68C‖	Change the column to 8 to start

E_C&a10C‖E_C&a+68C| printing two-digit line numbers.
E_C&a8C11E_C&a10C‖E_C&a+68C|
E_C&a10C‖E_C&a+68C|
E_C&a8C12E_C&a10C‖E_C&a+68C|
E_C&a10C‖E_C&a+68C|
E_C&a8C13E_C&a10C‖E_C&a+68C|
E_C&a10C‖E_C&a+68C|
E_C&a8C14E_C&a10C‖E_C&a+68C|
E_C&a10C‖E_C&a+68C|
E_C&a8C15E_C&a10C‖E_C&a+68C|
E_C&a10C‖E_C&a+68C|
E_C&a8C16E_C&a10C‖E_C&a+68C|
E_C&a10C‖E_C&a+68C|
E_C&a8C17E_C&a10C‖E_C&a+68C|
E_C&a10C‖E_C&a+68C|
E_C&a8C18E_C&a10C‖E_C&a+68C|
E_C&a10C‖E_C&a+68C|
E_C&a8C19E_C&a10C‖E_C&a+68C|
E_C&a10C‖E_C&a+68C|
E_C&a8C20E_C&a10C‖E_C&a+68C|
E_C&a10C‖E_C&a+68C|
E_C&a8C21E_C&a10C‖E_C&a+68C|
E_C&a10C‖E_C&a+68C|
E_C&a8C22E_C&a10C‖E_C&a+68C|
E_C&a10C‖E_C&a+68C|
E_C&a8C23E_C&a10C‖E_C&a+68C|
E_C&a10C‖E_C&a+68C|
E_C&a8C24E_C&a10C‖E_C&a+68C|
E_C&a10C‖E_C&a+68C|
E_C&a8C25E_C&a10C‖E_C&a+68C|
E_C&a10C‖E_C&a+68C|
E_C&a8C26E_C&a10C‖E_C&a+68C|

E_C&a10C‖E_C&a+68C| Extend the double and horizontal
E_C&a10C‖E_C&a+68C| vertical lines to near the bottom of the
E_C&a10C‖E_C&a+68C| page.
E_C&f1x4x10X   End the macro definition, enable the
macro for automatic overlay and make
the macro permanent.

Enter this series of PCL sequences into a new document, and save it as an ASCII file with an appropriate name, such as PLEAD.MAC. For more details about creating macros, refer to the examples in Chapter 5 of this book and the *Hewlett-Packard LaserJet Printer Technical Reference Manual.*

Although this command sequence is quite long, the commands are straightforward and repeated a number of times. Note that for compactness, the commands are combined. See Chapter 3 for more details about combining commands.

The macro is set up specifically to take advantage of carriage returns; if you alter the position of the carriage returns by typing the commands continuously so they run across the page, the sequence probably won't work correctly. The command pairs for drawing the double and single vertical bars on the pleading document are joined by the line numbering commands after the fifth pair. Notice also that the line numbers tend to blend into the command string.

If you understand the PCL programming sufficiently, you may want to shorten this sequence by eliminating all of the character-oriented double and vertical lines, and replacing them with PCL box drawing commands to draw the lines. Chapter 10 shows how to use the PCL Box command to draw a box one dot wide, which produces a printed line.

Downloading the Pleading Macro

To use the macro you just created, you must first download the macro from the PC to the LaserJet printer. To accomplish this from DOS, enter the command COPY PLEAD.MAC PRN. This command copies the PLEAD.MAC file to the printer. Each time you turn the printer on, you have to enter this DOS command.

To automate the process of downloading the macro, put the DOS command in your AUTOEXEC.BAT file. Then, each time your PC is turned on the macro for your pleading document will be automatically downloaded, ready to use.

Now that the macro has been downloaded to the printer, you can call the macro by placing a calling sequence at the top of each page to be printed. The pages will have their lines numbered and will have the required vertical lines in the proper places.

Calling the Pleading Macro

Enter the following PCL command at the top of each page that you want numbered and lined as a pleading document:

Command	Explanation
E_C&f8y4X	This combined command establishes the macro id 8 for subsequent macro operations, and enables the macro for automatic overlay.

```
<-&f8y4XIn CONGRESS, July 4, 1776.

    The unanimous Declaration of the

    thirteen united States of America,

When in the course of human events it becomes

necessary for one people to dissolve the political

bands which have connected them with another, and

to assume among the powers of the earth, the

separate and equal station to which the Laws of
```

Figure 7-7. PCL sequence at the top of the Declaration of Independence.

When you include this macro at the top of your legal documents, they will print with line numbers down the left margin and ruled lines in both margins.

1	In CONGRESS, July 4, 1776.
2	The unanimous Declaration of the
3	thirteen united States of America,
4	When in the course of human events it becomes
5	necessary for one people to dissolve the political
6	bands which have connected them with another, and
7	to assume among the powers of the earth, the
8	separate and equal station to which the Laws of

Figure 7-8. Declaration of Independence on a pleading document.

Before You Print

In order for this macro to work properly, here are some guidelines.

Use the HPPCCOUR.PRD driver for best results, with the Y-Cartridge and the PC1 character set.

Line spacing should be set to two lines per inch, and the margins as follows:

Left	1.25 inches
Top	1.5 inches
Right	.5 inches

Once the macro for the pleading document is complete, place the DOS downloading command in your AUTOEXEC.BAT file. The macro will then be downloaded to the printer each time you start the computer and will make using the macro as simple as choosing a command from your word processing program. In short, you'll be able to print pleading documents without much effort at all.

HP LASERJET AND MULTIMATE

In this example you'll create a PCL macro for printing the pleading document. After writing the macro, you'll save it in a file for future use. You'll also see how to download the macro to the LaserJet, and then call it for printing pleading documents from MultiMate.

Creating the Macro for a Pleading Document

The macro to print the pleading document contains the commands for printing line numbers and vertical lines down the side of each page. Here's the PCL sequence for the macro:

Command	Explanation
E_C&f8y0X	Establish a Macro ID and start the
E_C&a10C‖E_C&a+68C‖	Macro definition. Move the horizontal
E_C&a10C‖E_C&a+68C‖	cursor to column 10 and print the
E_C&a10C‖E_C&a+68C‖	double vertical line. Then move to
E_C&a10C‖E_C&a+68C‖	column 68 and print the single vertical
E_C&a10C‖E_C&a+68C‖	line. The carriage returns at the end of
	each command pair takes care of
	vertical cursor positioning.
E_C&a9C1E_C&a10C‖E_C&a+68C‖	Move the horizontal cursor to column
E_C&a10C‖E_C&a+68C‖	9 and print the line number.
E_C&a9C2E_C&a10C‖E_C&a+68C‖	Repeat the double and single
E_C&a10C‖E_C&a+68C‖	verticalline commands.
E_C&a9C3E_C&a10C‖E_C&a+68C‖	This command sequence
E_C&a10C‖E_C&a+68C‖	repeats through line 26.
E_C&a9C4E_C&a10C‖E_C&a+68C‖	
E_C&a10C‖E_C&a+68C‖	
E_C&a9C5E_C&a10C‖E_C&a+68C‖	
E_C&a10C‖E_C&a+68C‖	
E_C&a9C6E_C&a10C‖E_C&a+68C‖	
E_C&a10C‖E_C&a+68C‖	
E_C&a9C7E_C&a10C‖E_C&a+68C‖	
E_C&a10C‖E_C&a+68C‖	
E_C&a9C8E_C&a10C‖E_C&a+68C‖	
E_C&a10C‖E_C&a+68C‖	
E_C&a9C9E_C&a10C‖E_C&a+68C‖	
E_C&a10C‖E_C&a+68C‖	

Ec&a8C10Ec&a10C‖Ec&a+68C‖	Change the column to 8 to start
Ec&a10C‖Ec&a+68C‖	printing two-digit line numbers.
Ec&a8C11Ec&a10C‖Ec&a+68C‖	
Ec&a10C‖Ec&a+68C‖	
Ec&a8C12Ec&a10C‖Ec&a+68C‖	
Ec&a10C‖Ec&a+68C‖	
Ec&a8C13Ec&a10C‖Ec&a+68C‖	
Ec&a10C‖Ec&a+68C‖	
Ec&a8C14Ec&a10C‖Ec&a+68C‖	
Ec&a10C‖Ec&a+68C‖	
Ec&a8C15Ec&a10C‖Ec&a+68C‖	
Ec&a10C‖Ec&a+68C‖	
Ec&a8C16Ec&a10C‖Ec&a+68C‖	
Ec&a10C‖Ec&a+68C‖	
Ec&a8C17Ec&a10C‖Ec&a+68C‖	
Ec&a10C‖Ec&a+68C‖	
Ec&a8C18Ec&a10C‖Ec&a+68C‖	
Ec&a10C‖Ec&a+68C‖	
Ec&a8C19Ec&a10C‖Ec&a+68C‖	
Ec&a10C‖Ec&a+68C‖	
Ec&a8C20Ec&a10C‖Ec&a+68C‖	
Ec&a10C‖Ec&a+68C‖	
Ec&a8C21Ec&a10C‖Ec&a+68C‖	
Ec&a10C‖Ec&a+68C‖	
Ec&a8C22Ec&a10C‖Ec&a+68C‖	
Ec&a10C‖Ec&a+68C‖	
Ec&a8C23Ec&a10C‖Ec&a+68C‖	
Ec&a10C‖Ec&a+68C‖	
Ec&a8C24Ec&a10C‖Ec&a+68C‖	
Ec&a10C‖Ec&a+68C‖	
Ec&a8C25Ec&a10C‖Ec&a+68C‖	
Ec&a10C‖Ec&a+68C‖	
Ec&a8C26Ec&a10C‖Ec&a+68C‖	
Ec&a10C‖Ec&a+68C‖	Extend the double and horizontal
Ec&a10C‖Ec&a+68C‖	vertical lines to near the bottom of the
Ec&a10C‖Ec&a+68C‖	page.
Ec&f1x4x10X	End the macro definition, enable the
	macro for automatic overlay and make
	the macro permanent.

Enter this series of PCL sequences into a new document, and save it as an ASCII file with an appropriate name, such as PLEAD.MAC. For more details about creating macros, refer to the examples in Chapter 5 of this book and the *Hewlett-Packard LaserJet Printer Technical Reference Manual.*

Although this command sequence is quite long, the commands are straightforward and repeated a number of times. Note that for compactness, the commands are combined. See Chapter 3 for more details about combining commands.

The macro is set up specifically to take advantage of carriage returns; if you alter the position of the carriage returns by typing the commands continuously so they run across the page, the sequence probably won't work correctly. The command pairs for drawing the double and single vertical bars on the pleading document are joined by the line numbering commands after the fifth pair. Notice also that the line numbers tend to blend into the command string.

If you understand the PCL programming sufficiently, you may want to shorten this sequence by eliminating all of the character-oriented double and vertical lines, and replacing them with PCL box drawing commands to draw the lines. Chapter 10 shows how to use the PCL Box command to draw a box one dot wide, which produces a printed line.

Downloading the Pleading Macro

To use the macro you just created, you must first download the macro from the PC to the LaserJet printer. To accomplish this from DOS, enter the command COPY PLEAD.MAC PRN. This command copies the PLEAD.MAC file to the printer. Each time you turn the printer on, you have to enter this DOS command.

To automate the process of downloading the macro, put the DOS command in your AUTOEXEC.BAT file. Then, each time your PC is turned on the macro for your pleading document will be automatically downloaded, ready to use.

Now that the macro has been downloaded to the printer, you can call the macro by placing a calling sequence at the top of each page to be printed. The pages will have their lines numbered and will have the required vertical lines in the proper places.

Calling the Pleading Macro

To use MultiMate for the macro, you have to modify the printer driver because, if you use a TTY driver, you can't use the margins, but if you use a formatted driver, you can't use escape characters. The solution is to modify a driver for use with the pleading macro. The goal is to place the following PCL sequence into the driver initialization sequence:

Command	Explanation
E_C&f8y4X	This combined command establishes the macro id 8 for subsequent macro operations, and enables the macro for automatic overlay.

First, run the Util.exe on the MultiMate Utilities disk. Use the Printer Tables editor (PF10) to modify a PAT (Printer Action Table) named LJETSF1. Enter the hexadecimal sequence "1B266638793458" (which is E_C&f8y4X) in the Printer Initialization field, which is the first field . Save this table with a new name, such as LJPLEAD. This will set up the printer for your pleading documents. For complete, step-by-step instructions see the *MultiMate Printer Guide.*

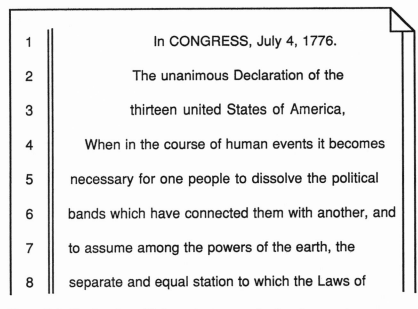

Figure 7-9. Declaration of Independence on a pleading document.

Before You Print

For best results, the Print Format Menu should specify the following:

Left Margin	12
Top Margin	7
Double Space	Yes (You can also specify this on the format line)
Pat	LJPLEAD

The right margin should be specified on the "Format Line" above the text, by moving the cursor to the position that you want as the end of the line, such as column 67.

Now, when you print your legal documents using the LJPLEAD.PAT driver, they will print with line numbers down the left margin and ruled lines in both margins.

Once the macro for the pleading document is complete, place the DOS downloading command in your AUTOEXEC.BAT file. The macro will then be downloaded to the printer each time you start the computer and will make using the macro as simple as choosing a command from your word processing program. In short, you'll be able to print pleading documents without much effort at all.

HP LASERJET AND WORDSTAR

In this example you'll create a PCL macro for printing the pleading document. After writing the macro, you'll save it in a file for future use. You'll also see how to download the macro to the LaserJet, and then call it for printing pleading documents from WordStar.

Creating the Macro for a Pleading Document

The macro to print the pleading document contains the commands for printing line numbers and vertical lines down the side of each page. Here's the PCL sequence for the macro:

<u>Command</u>	<u>Explanation</u>
E_C&f8y0X	Establish a Macro ID and start the
E_C&a10C‖E_C&a+68C|	Macro definition. Move the horizontal
E_C&a10C‖E_C&a+68C|	cursor to column 10 and print the
E_C&a10C‖E_C&a+68C|	double vertical line. Then move to
E_C&a10C‖E_C&a+68C|	column 68 and print the single vertical
E_C&a10C‖E_C&a+68C|	line. The carriage returns at the end of
	each command pair takes care of
	vertical cursor positioning.
E_C&a9C1E_C&a10C‖E_C&a+68C|	Move the horizontal cursor to column
E_C&a10C‖E_C&a+68C|	9 and print the line number.
E_C&a9C2E_C&a10C‖E_C&a+68C|	Repeat the double and single
E_C&a10C‖E_C&a+68C|	verticalline commands.
E_C&a9C3E_C&a10C‖E_C&a+68C|	This command sequence
E_C&a10C‖E_C&a+68C|	repeats through line 26.
E_C&a9C4E_C&a10C‖E_C&a+68C|	
E_C&a10C‖E_C&a+68C|	
E_C&a9C5E_C&a10C‖E_C&a+68C|	
E_C&a10C‖E_C&a+68C|	
E_C&a9C6E_C&a10C‖E_C&a+68C|	
E_C&a10C‖E_C&a+68C|	
E_C&a9C7E_C&a10C‖E_C&a+68C|	
E_C&a10C‖E_C&a+68C|	
E_C&a9C8E_C&a10C‖E_C&a+68C|	
E_C&a10C‖E_C&a+68C|	
E_C&a9C9E_C&a10C‖E_C&a+68C|	
E_C&a10C‖E_C&a+68C|	

E_C&a8C10E_C&a10C‖E_C&a+68C|
E_C&a10C‖E_C&a+68C|
E_C&a8C11E_C&a10C‖E_C&a+68C|
E_C&a10C‖E_C&a+68C|
E_C&a8C12E_C&a10C‖E_C&a+68C|
E_C&a10C‖E_C&a+68C|
E_C&a8C13E_C&a10C‖E_C&a+68C|
E_C&a10C‖E_C&a+68C|
E_C&a8C14E_C&a10C‖E_C&a+68C|
E_C&a10C‖E_C&a+68C|
E_C&a8C15E_C&a10C‖E_C&a+68C|
E_C&a10C‖E_C&a+68C|
E_C&a8C16E_C&a10C‖E_C&a+68C|
E_C&a10C‖E_C&a+68C|
E_C&a8C17E_C&a10C‖E_C&a+68C|
E_C&a10C‖E_C&a+68C|
E_C&a8C18E_C&a10C‖E_C&a+68C|
E_C&a10C‖E_C&a+68C|
E_C&a8C19E_C&a10C‖E_C&a+68C|
E_C&a10C‖E_C&a+68C|
E_C&a8C20E_C&a10C‖E_C&a+68C|
E_C&a10C‖E_C&a+68C|
E_C&a8C21E_C&a10C‖E_C&a+68C|
E_C&a10C‖E_C&a+68C|
E_C&a8C22E_C&a10C‖E_C&a+68C|
E_C&a10C‖E_C&a+68C|
E_C&a8C23E_C&a10C‖E_C&a+68C|
E_C&a10C‖E_C&a+68C|
E_C&a8C24E_C&a10C‖E_C&a+68C|
E_C&a10C‖E_C&a+68C|
E_C&a8C25E_C&a10C‖E_C&a+68C|
E_C&a10C‖E_C&a+68C|
E_C&a8C26E_C&a10C‖E_C&a+68C|
E_C&a10C‖E_C&a+68C|
E_C&a10C‖E_C&a+68C|
E_C&a10C‖E_C&a+68C|
E_C&f1x4x10X

Change the column to 8 to start printing two-digit line numbers.

Extend the double and horizontal vertical lines to near the bottom of the page.

End the macro definition, enable the macro for automatic overlay and make the macro permanent.

Enter this series of PCL sequences into a new document, and save it as an ASCII file with an appropriate name such as PLEAD.MAC. For more details about creating macros, refer to the examples in Chapter 5 of this book and the *Hewlett-Packard LaserJet Printer Technical Reference Manual*.

Although this command sequence is quite long, the commands are straightforward and repeated a number of times. Note that for compactness, the commands are combined. See Chapter 3 for more details about combining commands.

The macro is set up specifically to take advantage of carriage returns; if you alter the position of the carriage returns by typing the commands continuously so they run across the page, the sequence probably won't work correctly. The command pairs for drawing the double and single vertical bars on the pleading document are joined by the line numbering commands after the fifth pair. Notice also that the line numbers tend to blend into the command string.

If you understand the PCL programming sufficiently, you may want to shorten this sequence by eliminating all of the character-oriented double and vertical lines, and replacing them with PCL box drawing commands to draw the lines. Chapter 10 shows how to use the PCL Box command to draw a box one dot wide, which produces a printed line.

Downloading the Pleading Macro

To use the macro you just created, you must first download the macro from the PC to the LaserJet printer. To accomplish this from DOS, enter the command COPY PLEAD.MAC PRN. This command copies the PLEAD.MAC file to the printer. Each time you turn the printer on, you have to enter this DOS command.

To automate the process of downloading the macro, put the DOS command in your AUTOEXEC.BAT file. Then, each time your PC is turned on the macro for your pleading document will be automatically downloaded, ready to use.

Now that the macro has been downloaded to the printer, you can call the macro by placing a calling sequence at the top of each page to be printed. The pages will have their lines numbered and will have the required vertical lines in the proper places.

Calling the Pleading Macro

Enter the following PCL command at the top of each page that you want numbered and lined as a pleading document:

Command	Explanation
E_C&f8y4X	This combined command establishes the macro id 8 for subsequent macro operations, and enables the macro for automatic overlay.

```
<-&f8y4XIn CONGRESS, July 4, 1776.

    The unanimous Declaration of the

    thirteen united States of America,

When in the course of human events it becomes

necessary for one people to dissolve the political

bands which have connected them with another, and

to assume among the powers of the earth, the

separate and equal station to which the Laws of
```

Figure 7-10. PCL sequence at the top of the Declaration of Independence.

When you include this macro at the top of your legal documents, they will print with line numbers down the left margin and ruled lines in both margins.

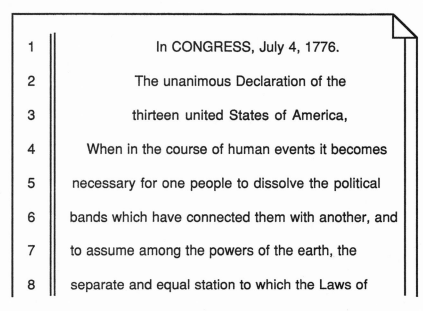

Figure 7-11. Declaration of Independence on a pleading document.

Before You Print

In order for this macro to work properly, here are some guidelines. For best results, use the .LS2 command for double spacing, and the .PA command wherever you want a page break. You should use a Control-B in each paragraph when you want to change the formatting. When printing your document, use Form Feeds = YES and DRAFT printer.

Once the macro for the pleading document is complete, place the DOS downloading command in your AUTOEXEC.BAT file. The macro will then be downloaded to the printer each time you start the computer and will make using the macro as simple as choosing a command from your word processing program. In short, you'll be able to print pleading documents without much effort at all.

Chapter 8

Drawing Horizontal Rules

Horizontal lines, or rules as they are called in the publishing business, are often used to separate the body of the text from footnotes, or to embellish the text at the end of a chapter. In this section, you'll learn how to create horizontal rules of various weights (thicknesses) and lengths. You'll also learn the details for placing the rules just where you want them in the text of your document.

KYOCERA AND MICROSOFT WORD

WORD has a built in feature for placing rules in your document. However, unlike a continuous inked line you expect to see in a professionally published document, the lines are actually composed of a series of repeating characters such as underscores and vertical bars connected together to form the rule.

Although the rules look reasonably well, being formed by repeating a series of underscores limits the choice of width or "weight" and restricts the placement of the lines to the usual positions for text. That is, the lines can't be anywhere outside of the normal areas for text. Fortunately, Prescribe has a good set of line drawing commands to overcome both limitations.

In the next two examples, you'll learn how to place a horizontal rule in your document just where you want it. You'll also learn how to make the rule different weights and lengths.

Placing a Horizontal Rule on the Left Margin

Here are the Prescribe commands needed to draw the rule:

Command	Explanation
!R!	staRt Prescribe sequence
UNIT I;	Set UNIT of measurement to inches
SPD .05;	Set Pen Diameter (width) to .05 inches
DRP 2,0;	Draw to Relative Position a horizontal rule 2 inches long from left margin. The 2 is called the X parameter because it controls the distance along the horizontal, or X-axis. The 0 is the Y parameter because it controls the distance vertically, or along the y-axis.
EXIT;	EXIT the Prescribe sequence

This Prescribe sequence will draw a horizontal rule .05 inches thick and two inches long, starting at the left margin as shown below.

```
ORLANDO. I attend them with all respect and
duty.

ROSALIND.(1) Young man, have you challenged
Charles the wrestler?

ORLANDO. No, fair princess: he is the general
challenger. I come but in, as others do, to try
with him the strength of my youth.

!R!UNIT I;SPD .05;DRP 2,0;EXIT;

1. Daughter of the banished Duke
```

Figure 8-1. Prescribe Sequence for Horizontal Rule in WORD. Notice the space before and after the sequence, and the corresponding space in the printed text.

ORLANDO. I attend them with all respect and duty.

ROSALIND.(1) Young man, have you challenged Charles the wrestler?

ORLANDO. No, fair princess: he is the general challenger. I come but in, as others do. to try with him the strength of my youth.

———

1. Daughter of the banished Duke

Figure 8-2. Printed Horizontal Rule. If you want the rule and footnote at the bottom of the page, add returns prior to the sequence as necessary.

Because drawing a rule is a relatively simple task, this Prescribe sequence is very short. As you can see in the figures, the rule prints at the same location where the code appeared within the text on the screen. Thus, you can place this horizontal rule sequence between the two parts of the text that you want the rule to separate.

To place the rule in your text, type all of the Prescribe commands on one line with semicolons separating each command, like this:

!R! UNIT I; SPD .05; DRP 2,0; EXIT;

By entering the entire sequence on one line, WORD will repaginate correctly, providing the extra line before and after the rule. If you want extra white space before or after the line, just add carriage returns before and after the line that holds the Prescribe commands.

Now, if you want to use this set of commands in your own text, here are some parameters to adjust to fit your own circumstances. The weight of the rule is set by the SPD command, from .0033 inches (just a hairline), to almost 1/2 inch thick, at .42 inches. The length of the line can also be varied by placing the length in inches in the X parameter of the DRP command. Note that in horizontal rules the Y parameter is unused and is always set to zero.

Placing a Centered Horizontal Rule

To move the rule to the center of the page, such as a centered rule near the end of the page to signify the end of a chapter, add an MRP command just before the SPD command:

!R! UNIT I; **MRP 1.75,0;** SPD .05; DRP 2,0; EXIT;

Again, the Y parameter in the MRP command is zero, but you need to calculate the X parameter to center the line. In the case of a 2-inch rule centered on the physical center of an 8.5-inch wide page with a 1.5-inch margin on the left, the formula would be: (page width / 2) - (line length / 2) - left margin: (8.5 / 2) - (2 / 2) - 1.5 = 1.75 inches. Although this seems a bit difficult, try a few examples to get the hang of it. The results will add a professional touch to your documents.

Using these simple commands, you can conveniently place publication quality rules in your text exactly where you want them. You'll be able to select the line's weight and length in order to enhance the readability and attractiveness of your documents.

```
The love I dedicate to your lordship is without
end: whereof this pamphlet, without beginning is
but a superfluous moiety. The warrant I have of
your honourable disposition, not the worth of my
untutored lines, make it assured of acceptance.
What I have done is yours; what I have to do is
yours; being part in all I have, devoted yours.
Were my worth greater, my duty would show great-
er; meantime, as it is, it is bound to your
lordship, to whom I wish long life still length-
ened with all happiness.

                        Your lordship's in all duty,
                            William Shakespeare

!R!UNIT I;MRP 1.75,0;SPD .05;DRP 2,0;EXIT;
```

Figure 8-3. Prescribe Sequence for Centered Horizontal Rule in WORD.

The love I dedicate to your lordship is without end: whereof this pamphlet, without beginning is but a superfluous moiety. The warrant I have of your honourable disposition, not the worth of my untutored lines, make it assured of acceptance. What I have done is yours; what I have to do is yours; being part in all I have, devoted yours. Were my worth greater, my duty would show greater; meantime, as it is, it is bound to your lordship, to whom I wish long life still lengthened with all happiness.

Your lordship's in all duty,
William Shakespeare

Figure 8-4. Printed Centered Horizontal Rule. If you want the rule at the bottom of the page, add carriage returns prior to the sequence as necessary.

KYOCERA AND MULTIMATE

MultiMate II has a built in feature for placing rules in your document. However, unlike a continuous inked line you expect to see in a professionally published document, the lines are actually composed of a series of repeating characters such as underscores and vertical bars connected together to form the rule.

Although the rules look reasonably well, being formed by repeating a series of underscores limits the choice of width or "weight" and restricts the placement of the lines to the usual positions for text. That is, the lines can't be anywhere outside of the normal areas for text. Fortunately, Prescribe has a good set of line drawing commands to overcome both limitations.

In the next two examples, you'll learn how to place a horizontal rule in your document just where you want it. You'll also learn how to make the rule different weights and lengths.

Placing a Horizontal Rule on the Left Margin

Here are the Prescribe commands needed to draw the rule:

Command	Explanation
!R!	staRt Prescribe sequence
UNIT I;	Set UNIT of measurement to inches
SPD .05;	Set Pen Diameter (width) to .05 inches
DRP 2,0;	Draw to Relative Position a horizontal rule 2 inches long from left margin. The 2 is called the X parameter because it controls the distance along the horizontal, or X-axis. The 0 is the Y parameter because it controls the distance vertically, or along the y-axis.
EXIT;	EXIT the Prescribe sequence

This Prescribe sequence will draw a horizontal rule .05 inches thick and two inches long, starting at the left margin as shown below.

```
ORLANDO. I attend them with all respect and
duty.

ROSALIND.(1) Young man, have you challenged
Charles the wrestler?

ORLANDO. No, fair princess: he is the general
challenger. I come but in, as others do, to try
with him the strength of my youth.

!R!UNIT I;SPD .05;DRP 2,0;EXIT;

1. Daughter of the banished Duke
```

Figure 8-5. Prescribe Sequence for Horizontal Rule in MultiMate. Notice the space before and after the sequence, and the corresponding space in the printed text.

ORLANDO. I attend them with all respect and duty.

ROSALIND.(1) Young man, have you challenged Charles the wrestler?

ORLANDO. No, fair princess: he is the general challenger. I come but in, as others do, to try with him the strength of my youth.

———————

1. Daughter of the banished Duke

Figure 8-6. Printed Horizontal Rule. If you want the rule and footnote at the bottom of the page, add returns prior to the sequence as necessary.

Because drawing a rule is a relatively simple task, this Prescribe sequence is very short. As you can see in the figures, the rule prints at the same location where the code appeared within the text on the screen. Thus, you can place this horizontal rule sequence between the two parts of the text that you want the rule to separate.

To place the rule in your text, type all of the Prescribe commands on one line with semicolons separating each command, like this:

!R! UNIT I; SPD .05; DRP 2,0; EXIT;

By entering the entire sequence on one line, MultiMate will repaginate correctly, providing the extra line before and after the rule. If you want extra white space before or after the line, just add carriage returns before and after the line that holds the Prescribe commands.

Now, if you want to use this set of commands in your own text, here are some parameters to adjust to fit your own circumstances. The weight of the rule is set by the SPD command, from .0033 inches (just a hairline), to almost 1/2 inch thick, at .42 inches. The length of the line can also be varied by placing the length in inches in the X parameter of the DRP command. Note that in horizontal rules the Y parameter is unused and is always set to zero.

Placing a Centered Horizontal Rule

To move the rule to the center of the page, such as a centered rule near the end of the page to signify the end of a chapter, add an MRP command just before the SPD command:

!R! UNIT I; **MRP 1.75,0;** SPD .05; DRP 2,0; EXIT;

Again, the Y parameter in the MRP command is zero, but you need to calculate the X parameter to center the line. In the case of a 2-inch rule centered on the physical center of an 8.5-inch wide page with a 1.5-inch margin on the left, the formula would be: (page width / 2) - (line length / 2) - left margin: $(8.5 / 2) - (2 / 2) - 1.5 = 1.75$ inches. Although this seems a bit difficult, try a few examples to get the hang of it. The results will add a professional touch to your documents.

Using these simple commands, you can conveniently place publication quality rules in your text exactly where you want them. You'll be able to select the line's weight and length in order to enhance the readability and attractiveness of your documents.

```
The love I dedicate to your lordship is without
end: whereof this pamphlet, without beginning is
but a superfluous moiety. The warrant I have of
your honourable disposition, not the worth of my
untutored lines, make it assured of acceptance.
What I have done is yours; what I have to do is
yours; being part in all I have, devoted yours.
Were my worth greater, my duty would show great-
er; meantime, as it is, it is bound to your
lordship, to whom I wish long life still length-
ened with all happiness.

                        Your lordship's in all duty,
                             William Shakespeare

!R!UNIT I;MRP 1.75,0;SPD .05;DRP 2,0;EXIT;
```

Figure 8-7. Prescribe Sequence for Centered Horizontal Rule in MultiMate.

The love I dedicate to your lordship is without end: whereof this pamphlet, without beginning is but a superfluous moiety. The warrant I have of your honourable disposition, not the worth of my untutored lines, make it assured of acceptance. What I have done is yours; what I have to do is yours; being part in all I have, devoted yours. Were my worth greater, my duty would show greater; meantime, as it is, it is bound to your lordship, to whom I wish long life still lengthened with all happiness.

Your lordship's in all duty,
William Shakespeare

Figure 8-8. Printed Centered Horizontal Rule. If you want the rule at the bottom of the page, add carriage returns prior to the sequence as necessary.

KYOCERA AND WORDSTAR

WordStar has a built in feature for placing rules in your document. However, unlike a continuous inked line you expect to see in a professionally published document, the lines are actually composed of a series of repeating characters such as underscores and vertical bars connected together to form the rule.

Although the rules look reasonably well, being formed by repeating a series of underscores limits the choice of width or "weight" and restricts the placement of the lines to the usual positions for text. That is, the lines can't be anywhere outside of the normal areas for text. Fortunately, Prescribe has a good set of line drawing commands to overcome both limitations.

In the next two examples, you'll learn how to place a horizontal rule in your document just where you want it. You'll also learn how to make the rule different weights and lengths.

Placing a Horizontal Rule on the Left Margin

Here are the Prescribe commands needed to draw the rule:

Command	Explanation
!R!	staRt Prescribe sequence
UNIT I;	Set UNIT of measurement to inches
SPD .05;	Set Pen Diameter (width) to .05 inches
DRP 2,0;	Draw to Relative Position a horizontal rule 2 inches long from left margin. The 2 is called the X parameter because it controls the distance along the horizontal, or X-axis. The 0 is the Y parameter because it controls the distance vertically, or along the y-axis.
EXIT;	EXIT the Prescribe sequence

This Prescribe sequence will draw a horizontal rule .05 inches thick and two inches long, starting at the left margin as shown below.

```
ORLANDO. I attend them with all respect and
duty.

ROSALIND.(1) Young man, have you challenged
Charles the wrestler?

ORLANDO. No, fair princess: he is the general
challenger. I come but in, as others do, to try
with him the strength of my youth.

!R!UNIT I;SPD .05;DRP 2,0;EXIT;

1. Daughter of the banished Duke
```

Figure 8-9. Prescribe Sequence for Horizontal Rule in WordStar. Notice the space before and after the sequence, and the corresponding space in the printed text.

ORLANDO. I attend them with all respect and duty.

ROSALIND.(1) Young man, have you challenged Charles the wrestler?

ORLANDO. No, fair princess: he is the general challenger. I come but in, as others do, to try with him the strength of my youth.

_____

1. Daughter of the banished Duke

Figure 8-10. Printed Horizontal Rule. If you want the rule and footnote at the bottom of the page, add returns prior to the sequence as necessary.

Because drawing a rule is a relatively simple task, this Prescribe sequence is very short. As you can see in the figures, the rule prints at the same location where the code appeared within the text on the screen. Thus, you can place this horizontal rule sequence between the two parts of the text that you want the rule to separate.

To place the rule in your text, type all of the Prescribe commands on one line with semicolons separating each command, like this:

!R! UNIT I; SPD .05; DRP 2,0; EXIT;

By entering the entire sequence on one line, WordStar will repaginate correctly, providing the extra line before and after the rule. If you want extra white space before or after the line, just add carriage returns before and after the line that holds the Prescribe commands.

Now, if you want to use this set of commands in your own text, here are some parameters to adjust to fit your own circumstances. The weight of the rule is set by the SPD command, from .0033 inches (just a hairline), to almost 1/2 inch thick, at .42 inches. The length of the line can also be varied by placing the length in inches in the X parameter of the DRP command. Note that in horizontal rules the Y parameter is unused and is always set to zero.

Placing a Centered Horizontal Rule

To move the rule to the center of the page, such as a centered rule near the end of the page to signify the end of a chapter, add an MRP command just before the SPD command:

!R! UNIT I; **MRP 1.75,0;** SPD .05; DRP 2,0; EXIT;

Again, the Y parameter in the MRP command is zero, but you need to calculate the X parameter to center the line. In the case of a 2-inch rule centered on the physical center of an 8.5-inch wide page with a 1.5-inch margin on the left, the formula would be: (page width / 2) - (line length / 2) - left margin: (8.5 / 2) - (2 / 2) - 1.5 = 1.75 inches. Although this seems a bit difficult, try a few examples to get the hang of it. The results will add a professional touch to your documents.

Using these simple commands, you can conveniently place publication quality rules in your text exactly where you want them. You'll be able to select the line's weight and length in order to enhance the readability and attractiveness of your documents.

```
The love I dedicate to your lordship is without
end: whereof this pamphlet, without beginning is
but a superfluous moiety. The warrant I have of
your honourable disposition, not the worth of my
untutored lines, make it assured of acceptance.
What I have done is yours; what I have to do is
yours; being part in all I have, devoted yours.
Were my worth greater, my duty would show great-
er; meantime, as it is, it is bound to your
lordship, to whom I wish long life still length-
ened with all happiness.

                         Your lordship's in all duty,
                            William Shakespeare

!R!UNIT I;MRP 1.75,0;SPD .05;DRP 2,0;EXIT;
```

Figure 8-11. Prescribe Sequence for Centered Horizontal Rule in WordStar.

The love I dedicate to your lordship is without end:
whereof this pamphlet, without beginning is but a
superfluous moiety. The warrant I have of your
honourable disposition, not the worth of my untutored
lines, make it assured of acceptance. What I have done is
yours; what I have to do is yours; being part in all I have,
devoted yours. Were my worth greater, my duty would
show greater; meantime, as it is, it is bound to your
lordship, to whom I wish long life still lengthened with
all happiness.

Your lordship's in all duty,
William Shakespeare

Figure 8-12. Printed Centered Horizontal Rule. If you want the rule at the bottom of the page, add carriage returns prior to the sequence as necessary.

HP LASERJET AND MICROSOFT WORD

WORD has a built in feature for placing rules in your document. However, unlike a continuous inked line you expect to see in a professionally published document, the lines are actually composed of a series of repeating characters such as underscores and vertical bars connected together to form the rule.

Although the rules look reasonably well, being formed by repeating a series of underscores limits the choice of width or "weight" and restricts the placement of the lines to the usual positions for text. That is, the lines can't be anywhere outside of the normal areas for text. Fortunately, PCL has a set of line drawing commands to overcome both limitations.

In the next two examples, you'll learn how to place a horizontal rule in your document just where you want it. You'll also learn how to make the rule different weights and lengths.

Placing a Horizontal Rule on the Left Margin

PCL does not have a specific line drawing command like Prescribe for the Kyocera. The example below uses the rectangle drawing command instead to achieve the same goal. In other words, the PCL commands draws a box which has overlapping sides, so it is essentially a single, thick line. Here are the PCL commands needed to draw the rule:

Command	Explanation
E_C*c600A	Set rectangle width to 600 dots - 2 inches
E_C*c15B	Set rectangle depth to 15 dots - .05 inches
E_C*c0P	Draw the specified rectangle

This PCL sequence will draw a rectangle which looks like a horizontal rule .05 inches thick and two inches long, starting at the left margin.

```
ORLANDO. I attend them with all respect and
duty.

ROSALIND.(1) Young man, have you challenged
Charles the wrestler?

ORLANDO. No, fair princess: he is the general
challenger. I come but in, as others do, to try
with him the strength of my youth.

<-*c600A<-*c15B<-*c0P
1. Daughter of the banished Duke
```

Figure 8-13. PCL Sequence for Horizontal Rule in WORD. Notice the space only before the sequence, and the corresponding space in the printed text.

ORLANDO. I attend them with all respect and duty.

ROSALIND.(1) Young man, have you challenged Charles the wrestler?

ORLANDO. No, fair princess: he is the general challenger. I come but in, as others do, to try with him the strength of my youth.

———————

1. Daughter of the banished Duke

Figure 8-14. Printed Horizontal Rule. If you want the rule and footnote at the bottom of the page, add returns prior to the sequence as necessary.

Because drawing a rule is a relatively simple task, this PCL sequence is very short. As you can see in the figures, the rule prints at the same location where the code appeared within the text on the screen. Thus, you can place this horizontal rule sequence between the two parts of the text that you want the rule to separate.

To place the rule in your text, type each of the PCL commands on one line, like this:

E_C*c600AE_C*c15BE_C*c0P

By entering the entire sequence on one line, WORD will repaginate correctly, providing the extra line before and after the rule. If you want extra white space before or after the line, add carriage returns above and below the line that holds the sequence.

Now, if you want to use this set of commands in your own document, here are some parameters to adjust to fit your own circumstances. The length of the rule is set by the first command(E_C*c600A), using dots per inch. In this case, 600 dots equals 2 inches because the Laserjet prints 300 dots per inch. Likewise, the width can also be varied by changing the dots per inch in the second command (E_C*c15B). Here it is set at 15 dots, or .05 inches (15 divided by 300 equals .05). After you set the width and length of the rectangle, the final command (E_C*c0P) is the one that does the drawing.

Placing a Centered Horizontal Rule

To move the rule to the center of the page, such as a centered rule near the end of the page to signify the end of a chapter, you add another command right after the escape character:

E_C**p525X**E_C*c600AE_C*c15BE_C*c0P

The new PCL command (in boldface) is the horizontal cursor position command. The number 525 is 1.75 inches at 300 dots per inch. The 1.75 inches is the amount of space to move the cursor to the right before starting to draw the line. To calculate how far to move the cursor to the right for a 2-inch rule centered on the physical center of an 8.5-inch wide page with a 1.5-nch margin on the left, the formula would be: (page width / 2) - (line length / 2) - left margin, or (8.5 / 2) - (2 / 2) - 1.5 = 1.75 inches. Then to find the setting for the PCL command multiply 300 by 1.75, which equals 525.

Using these commands, you can conveniently place publication quality rules in your text exactly where you want them. You'll be able to select the line's

weight and length in order to enhance the readability and attractiveness of your documents.

```
The love I dedicate to your lordship is without
end: whereof this pamphlet, without beginning is
but a superfluous moiety. The warrant I have of
your honourable disposition, not the worth of my
untutored lines, make it assured of acceptance.
What I have done is yours; what I have to do is
yours; being part in all I have, devoted yours.
Were my worth greater, my duty would show great-
er; meantime, as it is, it is bound to your
lordship, to whom I wish long life still length-
ened with all happiness.

                        Your lordship's in all duty,
                             William Shakespeare

<-*p525X<-*c600A<-*c15B<-*c0P
```

Figure 8-15. PCL Sequence for Centered Horizontal Rule in WORD.

The love I dedicate to your lordship is without end: whereof this pamphlet, without beginning is but a superfluous moiety. The warrant I have of your honourable disposition, not the worth of my untutored lines, make it assured of acceptance. What I have done is yours; what I have to do is yours; being part in all I have, devoted yours. Were my worth greater, my duty would show greater; meantime, as it is, it is bound to your lordship, to whom I wish long life still lengthened with all happiness.

Your lordship's in all duty,
William Shakespeare

Figure 8-16. Printed Centered Horizontal Rule. If you want the rule at the bottom of the page, add carriage returns prior to the sequence as necessary.

HP LASERJET AND MULTIMATE

MultiMate has a built in feature for placing rules in your document. However, unlike a continuous inked line you expect to see in a professionally published document, the lines are actually composed of a series of repeating characters such as underscores and vertical bars connected together to form the rule.

Although the rules look reasonably well, being formed by repeating a series of underscores limits the choice of width or "weight" and restricts the placement of the lines to the usual positions for text. That is, the lines can't be anywhere outside of the normal areas for text. Fortunately, PCL has a set of line drawing commands to overcome both limitations.

In the next two examples, you'll learn how to place a horizontal rule in your document just where you want it. You'll also learn how to make the rule different weights and lengths.

Placing a Horizontal Rule on the Left Margin

PCL does not have a specific line drawing command like Prescribe for the Kyocera. The example below uses the rectangle drawing command instead to achieve the same goal. In other words, the PCL commands draws a box which has overlapping sides, so it is essentially a single, thick line. Here are the PCL commands needed to draw the rule:

Command	Explanation
E_C*c600A	Set rectangle width to 600 dots - 2 inches
E_C*c15B	Set rectangle depth to 15 dots - .05 inches
E_C*c0P	Draw the specified rectangle

This PCL sequence will draw a rectangle which looks like a horizontal rule .05 inches thick and two inches long, starting at the left margin.

```
ORLANDO. I attend them with all respect and
duty.

ROSALIND.(1) Young man, have you challenged
Charles the wrestler?

ORLANDO. No, fair princess: he is the general
challenger. I come but in, as others do, to try
with him the strength of my youth.

<-*c600A<-*c15B<-*c0P
1. Daughter of the banished Duke
```

Figure 8-17. PCL Sequence for Horizontal Rule in MultiMate. Notice the space only before the sequence, and the corresponding space in the printed text.

ORLANDO. I attend them with all respect and duty.

ROSALIND.(1) Young man, have you challenged Charles the wrestler?

ORLANDO. No, fair princess: he is the general challenger. I come but in, as others do, to try with him the strength of my youth.

1. Daughter of the banished Duke

Figure 8-18. Printed Horizontal Rule. If you want the rule and footnote at the bottom of the page, add returns prior to the sequence as necessary.

Because drawing a rule is a relatively simple task, this PCL sequence is very short. As you can see in the figures, the rule prints at the same location where the code appeared within the text on the screen. Thus, you can place this horizontal rule sequence between the two parts of the text that you want the rule to separate.

To place the rule in your text, type each of the PCL commands on one line, like this:

E_C*c600AE_C*c15BE_C*c0P

By entering the entire sequence on one line, MultiMate will repaginate correctly, providing the extra line before and after the rule. If you want extra white space before or after the line, add carriage returns above and below the line that holds the sequence.

Now, if you want to use this set of commands in your own document, here are some parameters to adjust to fit your own circumstances. The length of the rule is set by the first command(E_C*c600A), using dots per inch. In this case, 600 dots equals 2 inches because the Laserjet prints 300 dots per inch. Likewise, the width can also be varied by changing the dots per inch in the second command (E_C*c15B). Here it is set at 15 dots, or .05 inches (15 divided by 300 equals .05). After you set the width and length of the rectangle, the final command (E_C*c0P) is the one that does the drawing.

Placing a Centered Horizontal Rule

To move the rule to the center of the page, such as a centered rule near the end of the page to signify the end of a chapter, you add another command right after the escape character:

E_C**p525X**E_C*c600AE_C*c15BE_C*c0P

The new PCL command (in boldface) is the horizontal cursor position command. The number 525 is 1.75 inches at 300 dots per inch. The 1.75 inches is the amount of space to move the cursor to the right before starting to draw the line. To calculate how far to move the cursor to the right for a 2-inch rule centered on the physical center of an 8.5-inch wide page with a 1.5-inch margin on the left, the formula would be: (page width / 2) - (line length / 2) - left margin, or (8.5 / 2) - (2 / 2) - 1.5 = 1.75 inches. Then to find the setting for the PCL command multiply 300 by 1.75, which equals 525.

Using these commands, you can conveniently place publication quality rules in your text exactly where you want them. You'll be able to select the line's

weight and length in order to enhance the readability and attractiveness of your documents.

```
The love I dedicate to your lordship is without
end: whereof this pamphlet, without beginning is
but a superfluous moiety. The warrant I have of
your honourable disposition, not the worth of my
untutored lines, make it assured of acceptance.
What I have done is yours; what I have to do is
yours; being part in all I have, devoted yours.
Were my worth greater, my duty would show great-
er; meantime, as it is, it is bound to your
lordship, to whom I wish long life still length-
ened with all happiness.

                      Your lordship's in all duty,
                              William Shakespeare

<-*p525X<-*c600A<-*c15B<-*c0P
```

Figure 8-19. PCL Sequence for Centered Horizontal Rule in MultiMate.

The love I dedicate to your lordship is without end: whereof this pamphlet, without beginning is but a superfluous moiety. The warrant I have of your honourable disposition, not the worth of my untutored lines, make it assured of acceptance. What I have done is yours; what I have to do is yours; being part in all I have, devoted yours. Were my worth greater, my duty would show greater; meantime, as it is, it is bound to your lordship, to whom I wish long life still lengthened with all happiness.

Your lordship's in all duty,
William Shakespeare

Figure 8-20. Printed Centered Horizontal Rule. If you want the rule at the bottom of the page, add carriage returns prior to the sequence as necessary.

HP LASERJET AND WORDSTAR

WordStar has a built in feature for placing rules in your document. However, unlike a continuous inked line you expect to see in a professionally published document, the lines are actually composed of a series of repeating characters such as underscores and vertical bars connected together to form the rule.

Although the rules look reasonably well, being formed by repeating a series of underscores limits the choice of width or "weight" and restricts the placement of the lines to the usual positions for text. That is, the lines can't be anywhere outside of the normal areas for text. Fortunately, PCL has a set of line drawing commands to overcome both limitations.

In the next two examples, you'll learn how to place a horizontal rule in your document just where you want it. You'll also learn how to make the rule different weights and lengths.

Placing a Horizontal Rule on the Left Margin

PCL does not have a specific line drawing command like Prescribe for the Kyocera. The example below uses the rectangle drawing command instead to achieve the same goal. In other words, the PCL commands draws a box which has overlapping sides, so it is essentially a single, thick line. Here are the PCL commands needed to draw the rule:

Command	Explanation
E_C*c600A	Set rectangle width to 600 dots - 2 inches
E_C*c15B	Set rectangle depth to 15 dots - .05 inches
E_C*c0P	Draw the specified rectangle

This PCL sequence will draw a rectangle which looks like a horizontal rule .05 inches thick and two inches long, starting at the left margin.

```
ORLANDO. I attend them with all respect and
duty.

ROSALIND.(1) Young man, have you challenged
Charles the wrestler?

ORLANDO. No, fair princess: he is the general
challenger. I come but in, as others do, to try
with him the strength of my youth.

<-*c600A<-*c15B<-*c0P
1. Daughter of the banished Duke
```

Figure 8-21. PCL Sequence for Horizontal Rule in WordStar. Notice the space only before the sequence, and the corresponding space in the printed text.

ORLANDO. I attend them with all respect and duty.

ROSALIND.(1) Young man, have you challenged Charles the wrestler?

ORLANDO. No, fair princess: he is the general challenger. I come but in, as others do, to try with him the strength of my youth.

_____

1. Daughter of the banished Duke

Figure 8-22. Printed Horizontal Rule. If you want the rule and footnote at the bottom of the page, add returns prior to the sequence as necessary.

Because drawing a rule is a relatively simple task, this PCL sequence is very short. As you can see in the figures, the rule prints at the same location where the code appeared within the text on the screen. Thus, you can place this horizontal rule sequence between the two parts of the text that you want the rule to separate.

To place the rule in your text, type each of the PCL commands on one line, like this:

E_C*c600AE_C*c15BE_C*c0P

By entering the entire sequence on one line, WordStar will repaginate correctly, providing the extra line before and after the rule. If you want extra white space before or after the line, add carriage returns above and below the line that holds the sequence.

Now, if you want to use this set of commands in your own document, here are some parameters to adjust to fit your own circumstances. The length of the rule is set by the first command(E_C*c600A), using dots per inch. In this case, 600 dots equals 2 inches because the Laserjet prints 300 dots per inch. Likewise, the width can also be varied by changing the dots per inch in the second command (E_C*c15B). Here it is set at 15 dots, or .05 inches (15 divided by 300 equals .05). After you set the width and length of the rectangle, the final command (E_C*c0P) is the one that does the drawing.

Placing a Centered Horizontal Rule

To move the rule to the center of the page, such as a centered rule near the end of the page to signify the end of a chapter, you add another command right after the escape character:

E_C**p525X**E_C*c600AE_C*c15BE_C*c0P

The new PCL command (in boldface) is the horizontal cursor position command. The number 525 is 1.75 inches at 300 dots per inch. The 1.75 inches is the amount of space to move the cursor to the right before starting to draw the line. To calculate how far to move the cursor to the right for a 2-inch rule centered on the physical center of an 8.5-inch wide page with a 1.5-inch margin on the left, the formula would be: (page width / 2) - (line length / 2) - left margin, or (8.5 / 2) - (2 / 2) - 1.5 = 1.75 inches. Then to find the setting for the PCL command multiply 300 by 1.75, which equals 525.

Using these commands, you can conveniently place publication quality rules in your text exactly where you want them. You'll be able to select the line's

weight and length in order to enhance the readability and attractiveness of your documents.

```
The love I dedicate to your lordship is without
end: whereof this pamphlet, without beginning is
but a superfluous moiety. The warrant I have of
your honourable disposition, not the worth of my
untutored lines, make it assured of acceptance.
What I have done is yours; what I have to do is
yours; being part in all I have, devoted yours.
Were my worth greater, my duty would show great-
er; meantime, as it is, it is bound to your
lordship, to whom I wish long life still length-
ened with all happiness.

                        Your lordship's in all duty,
                             William Shakespeare

<-*p525X<-*c600A<-*c15B<-*c0P
```

Figure 8-23. PCL Sequence for Centered Horizontal Rule in WordStar.

The love I dedicate to your lordship is without end: whereof this pamphlet, without beginning is but a superfluous moiety. The warrant I have of your honourable disposition, not the worth of my untutored lines, make it assured of acceptance. What I have done is yours; what I have to do is yours; being part in all I have, devoted yours. Were my worth greater, my duty would show greater; meantime, as it is, it is bound to your lordship, to whom I wish long life still lengthened with all happiness.

Your lordship's in all duty,
William Shakespeare

Figure 8-24. Printed Centered Horizontal Rule. If you want the rule at the bottom of the page, add carriage returns prior to the sequence as necessary.

Chapter 9

Annotating Text with Vertical Lines

Vertical lines, or rules, are very useful for indicating where changes have occurred in different versions of a document. For example, a new edition of an instruction manual might highlight each changed paragraph with a vertical line in the left margin.

Another common use of vertical rules is to highlight some text that may be of special interest. You can further offset the text by indenting it both on the left and right, and then placing the rules on either side.

KYOCERA AND MICROSOFT WORD

The WORD feature for drawing vertical rules is the same one for drawing horizontal rules. And, just like horizontal rules, the vertical rules are built with characters, and the same limitations of rule weight, length, and placement apply. Thus, it's difficult to place a rule in the margin of your document.

WORD does contain a feature for marking revisions between drafts of a document, but using that feature adds some printing marks you may not want, such as underscores and strikethroughs. Furthermore, only the line with the changes is marked, not the entire paragraph.

To get vertical rules just as you want them as shown in the illustration, use the Prescribe language instead of WORD's feature.

```
Beauty, truth and rarity,
Grace in all simplicity,
Here enclosed, in cinders lie.

!R!;UNIT I;MRP -1,.1;SPD .02;DRP 0,.4;
MRP .1,-.5;EXIT;
Death is now the phoenix' nest;
And the turtle's loyal breast
To eternity doth rest.

Leaving no posterity,
'Twas not their infirmity,
It was married chastity.
```

Figure 9-1. Prescribe Sequence for Vertical Rule in WORD. The sequence is on two lines only for the purpose of this illustration.

> Beauty, truth and rarity,
> Grace in all simplicity,
> Here enclosed, in cinders lie.
>
> Death is now the phoenix' nest;
> And the turtle's loyal breast
> To eternity doth rest.
>
> Leaving no posterity,
> 'Twas not their infirmity,
> It was married chastity.

Figure 9-2. Printed Vertical Rule, used to annotate or highlight selected paragraphs.

Here are the Prescribe commands needed to draw a vertical rule:

Command	Explanation
!R!	staRt Prescribe sequence
UNIT I;	set UNIT of measurement to inches
MRP -.1,.1;	Move the Relative Position of cursor left .1 inch, and down .1 inch
SPD .02;	Set Pen Diameter to .02 inches
DRP 0,.4;	Draw Relative Pen vertically .4 inches
MRP .1,-.5;	Move the Relative Position of cursor right .1 inch and up .5 inch .
EXIT;	EXIT the Prescribe sequence

This Prescribe sequence will draw a vertical rule just to the left of the margin. As with the horizontal rule Prescribe sequence, place this sequence directly before the text you wish to highlihgt. Enter the Prescribe commands on one line with semicolons separating them, so that WORD will repaginate correctly. This is how the sequence should look on your screen:

!R! UNIT I; MRP -.1,.1; SPD .02; DRP 0,.4; MRP .1,-.5; EXIT;

Here's what this Prescribe sequence does: first, MRP moves the cursor into the left margin one tenth of an inch, and drops the cursor vertically one tenth of an inch. The reason for dropping the cursor is that most characters are not full height. Dropping the cursor aligns the rule to the characters and is aesthetically pleasing. If you don't see the value in this now, try a vertical bar without the adjustment. You'll probably find that small difference irritating.

Next, the SPD command sets the width of the pen to .02 inches. Then, the DRP command draws the line to the length specified by the .4 (which is the y parameter and controls vertical lengths). To calculate the length, multiply the height of the text—in this case approximately .167 inches (6 lines per inch) times 3 lines equals .501 inches. Next, subtract the previous adjustment for the .1 inch white space at the top of the first line, and round out to .4 inches.

Finally, the last MRP reverses the cursor positioning to put the cursor right back where the word processor left it, in preparation for printing.

This may seem like a lot of effort, but after you've practiced with a few lines, you'll come to enjoy the flexibility and value of your new skill and it will add to the appearance and readability of your documents.

KYOCERA AND MULTIMATE

The MultiMate feature for drawing vertical rules is the same one for drawing horizontal rules. And, just like horizontal rules, the vertical rules are built with characters, and the same limitations of rule weight, length, and placement apply. Thus, it's difficult to place a rule in the margin of your document.

To get vertical rules just as you want them as shown in the illustration, use the Prescribe language.

```
Beauty, truth and rarity,
Grace in all simplicity,
Here enclosed, in cinders lie.

!R!;UNIT I;MRP -1,.1;SPD .02;DRP 0,.4;
MRP .1,-.5;EXIT;
Death is now the phoenix' nest;
And the turtle's loyal breast
To eternity doth rest.

Leaving no posterity,
'Twas not their infirmity,
It was married chastity.
```

Figure 9-3. Prescribe Sequence for Vertical Rule in MultiMate. The sequence is on two lines only for the purpose of this illustration.

Beauty, truth and rarity,
Grace in all simplicity,
Here enclosed, in cinders lie.

Death is now the phoenix' nest;
And the turtle's loyal breast
To eternity doth rest.

Leaving no posterity,
'Twas not their infirmity,
It was married chastity.

Figure 9-4. Printed Vertical Rule, used to annotate or highlight selected paragraphs.

Here are the Prescribe commands needed to draw a vertical rule:

Command	Explanation
!R!	staRt Prescribe sequence
UNIT I;	set UNIT of measurement to inches
MRP -.1,.1;	Move the Relative Position of cursor left .1 inch, and down .1 inch
SPD .02;	Set Pen Diameter to .02 inches
DRP 0,.4;	Draw Relative Pen vertically .4 inches
MRP .1,-.5;	Move the Relative Position of cursor right .1 inch and up .5 inch .
EXIT;	EXIT the Prescribe sequence

This Prescribe sequence will draw a vertical rule just to the left of the margin. As with the horizontal rule Prescribe sequence, place this sequence directly before the text you wish to highlight. Simply enter the Prescribe commands on one line with semicolons separating them, so that MultiMate will repaginate correctly. This is how the sequence should look on your screen:

!R! UNIT I; MRP -.1,.1; SPD .02; DRP 0,.4; MRP .1,-.5; EXIT;

Here's what this Prescribe sequence does: first, MRP moves the cursor into the left margin one tenth of an inch, and drops the cursor vertically one tenth of an inch. The purpose for dropping the cursor may not be readily apparent, but remember that most characters are not full height. Dropping the cursor just a bit aligns the rule more accurately to the characters and is aesthetically pleasing. If you don't see the value in this extra effort now, try a vertical bar later on without the adjustment. You'll probably find that small difference irritating.

Next, the SPD command sets the width of the pen to .02 inches. Then, the DRP command draws the line to the length specified by the .4 (which is the y parameter and controls vertical lengths). To calculate the length, multiply the height of the text—in this case approximately .167 inches (6 lines per inch) times 3 lines equals .501 inches. Next, subtract the previous adjustment for the .1 inch white space at the top of the first line, and round out to .4 inches.

Finally, the last MRP reverses the cursor positioning parameters in order to put the cursor right back where the word processor left it, in preparation for printing the text.

All of this may seem like too much effort the first time through, but after you've practiced with a few lines, you'll come to enjoy the flexibility and value of your new skill and it will add to the appearance and readability of your documents.

KYOCERA AND WORDSTAR

The WordStar feature for drawing vertical rules is the same one for drawing horizontal rules. And, just like horizontal rules, the vertical rules are built with characters, and the same limitations of rule weight, length, and placement apply. Thus, it's difficult to place a rule in the margin of your document.

To get vertical rules just as you want them as shown in the illustration, use the Prescribe language instead.

```
Beauty, truth and rarity,
Grace in all simplicity,
Here enclosed, in cinders lie.

!R!;UNIT I;MRP -1,.1;SPD .02;DRP 0,.4;
MRP .1,-.5;EXIT;
Death is now the phoenix' nest;
And the turtle's loyal breast
To eternity doth rest.

Leaving no posterity,
'Twas not their infirmity,
It was married chastity.
```

Figure 9-5. Prescribe Sequence for Vertical Rule in WordStar. The sequence is on two lines only for the purpose of this illustration.

Beauty, truth and rarity,
Grace in all simplicity,
Here enclosed, in cinders lie.

Death is now the phoenix' nest;
And the turtle's loyal breast
To eternity doth rest.

Leaving no posterity,
'Twas not their infirmity,
It was married chastity.

Figure 9-6. Printed Vertical Rule, used to annotate or highlight selected paragraphs.

Here are the Prescribe commands needed to draw a vertical rule:

Command	Explanation
!R!	staRt Prescribe sequence
UNIT I;	set UNIT of measurement to inches
MRP -.1,.1;	Move the Relative Position of cursor left .1 inch, and down .1 inch
SPD .02;	Set Pen Diameter to .02 inches
DRP 0,.4;	Draw Relative Pen vertically .4 inches
MRP .1,-.5;	Move the Relative Position of cursor right .1 inch and up .5 inch .
EXIT;	EXIT the Prescribe sequence

This Prescribe sequence will draw a vertical rule just to the left of the margin. As with the horizontal rule Prescribe sequence, place this sequence directly before the text you wish to annotate. Simply enter the Prescribe commands on one line with semicolons separating them, so that WordStar will repaginate correctly. This is how the sequence should look on your screen:

!R! UNIT I; MRP -.1,.1; SPD .02; DRP 0,.4; MRP .1,-.5; EXIT;

Here's what this Prescribe sequence does: first, MRP moves the cursor into the left margin one tenth of an inch, and drops the cursor vertically one tenth of an inch. The purpose for dropping the cursor may not be readily apparent, but remember that most characters are not full height. Dropping the cursor just a bit aligns the rule more accurately to the characters and is aesthetically pleasing. If you don't see the value in this extra effort now, try a vertical bar later on without the adjustment. You'll probably find that small difference irritating.

Next, the SPD command sets the width of the pen to .02 inches. Then, the DRP command draws the line to the length specified by the .4 (which is the y parameter and controls vertical lengths). To calculate the length, multiply the height of the text—in this case approximately .167 inches (6 lines per inch) times 3 lines equals .501 inches. Next, subtract the previous adjustment for the .1 inch white space at the top of the first line, and round out to .4 inches.

Finally, the last MRP reverses the cursor positioning parameters in order to put the cursor right back where the word processor left it, in preparation for printing the text.

All of this may seem like too much effort the first time through, but after you've practiced with a few lines, you'll come to enjoy the flexibility and value of your new skill and it will add to the appearance and readability of your documents.

HP LASERJET AND MICROSOFT WORD

The WORD feature for drawing vertical rules is the same one for drawing horizontal rules. And, just like horizontal rules, the vertical rules are built with characters, and the same limitations of weight, length, and placement apply. Thus, it would be difficult to place a rule in the margin of your document. In the next example, you'll learn how to draw vertical rules in the left margin of your document with PCL commands.

PCL does not have a line drawing command like Prescribe. The example below uses the rectangle drawing command instead to achieve the same goal. Here are the PCL commands needed to draw the rule:

Command	Explanation
E_C&f0S	Save the current cursor position
E_C*p-30X	move cursor position left .1 inch
E_C*p+30Y	move cursor position down .1 inch
E_C*c6A	Set rectangle width to .02 inches (6 / 300 dots per inch = .02 inches)
E_C*c120B	Set rectangle depth to 120 dots, or .4 inches
E_C*c0P	Draw the specified rectangle
E_C&f1S	Restore the cursor position saved earlier

```
Beauty, truth and rarity,
Grace in all simplicity,
Here enclosed, in cinders lie.
<-&f0S<-*p-30X<-*p+30Y<-*c6A<-*c120B<-*c0P<-&f1S
Death is now the phoenix' nest;
And the turtle's loyal breast
To eternity doth rest.

Leaving no posterity,
'Twas not their infirmity,
It was married chastity.
```

Figure 9-7. PCL Sequence for Vertical Rule in WORD. Notice there are no spaces between the first and second stanza.

Beauty, truth and rarity,
Grace in all simplicity,
Here enclosed, in cinders lie.

Death is now the phoenix' nest;
And the turtle's loyal breast
To eternity doth rest.

Leaving no posterity,
'Twas not their infirmity,
It was married chastity.

Figure 9-8. Printed Vertical Rule, used to annotate or highlight selected paragraphs.

This PCL sequence will draw a vertical rule just to the left of the margin. Put the sequence in the text where you want the vertical line to begin. For instance, if you want to annotate a changed paragraph, put the sequence on the line preceding the paragraph. Enter the PCL commands on one line so that WORD will repaginate correctly. The sequence should look like this on your screen:

E_C&f0SE_C*p-30XE_C*p+30YE_C*c6AE_C*c120BE_C*c0PE_C&f1S

Here's what this sequence does: first, f0S saves the current position of the cursor, because you will need to return it to its starting point for subsequent text to be printed correctly. Then, the p- command moves the cursor into the left margin one tenth of an inch, and the p+ command drops the cursor vertically one tenth of an inch. The purpose for dropping the cursor is to align the beginning of the rule more accurately with the text characters. Although that alignment takes a little extra effort, it's aesthetically pleasing. Try a vertical bar without the adjustment and you'll probably see the vertical line as misaligned and irritating.

The next two c commands set the width and depth (length) of the rectangle. To calculate the length, multiply the height of the text —in this case approximately .167 inches (6 lines per inch) times 3 lines equals .501 inches.

Next, subtract the previous adjustment for the .1 inch white space at the top of the first line, and round out to .4 inches, or 120 dots.

The next command, c0P, draws the rectangle.

The last command in the sequence restores the cursor to its previously saved location in preparation for printing the text properly positioned.

All of this may seem like too much effort the first time through, but after you've practiced with a few lines, you'll come to enjoy the flexibility and value of your new skill. And it will add to the appearance and readability of your documents.

HP LASERJET AND MULTIMATE

The MultiMate feature for drawing vertical rules is the same one for drawing horizontal rules. But, just like horizontal rules, the vertical rules are also built with characters, and the same limitations of weight, length, and placement apply. Thus, it would be difficult to place a rule in the margin of your document. In the next example, you'll learn how to draw vertical rules in the left margin of your document with PCL commands.

PCL does not have a line drawing command like Prescribe. The example below uses the rectangle drawing command instead to achieve the same goal. Here are the PCL commands needed to draw the rule:

Command	Explanation
E_C&f0S	Save the current cursor position
E_C*p-30X	move cursor position left .1 inch
E_C*p+30Y	move cursor position down .1 inch
E_C*c6A	Set rectangle width to .02 inches
	(6 / 300 dots per inch = .02 inches)
E_C*c120B	Set rectangle depth to 120 dots, or .4 inches
E_C*c0P	Draw the specified rectangle
E_C&f1S	Restore the cursor position saved earlier

```
Beauty, truth and rarity,
Grace in all simplicity,
Here enclosed, in cinders lie.
<-&f0S<-*p-30X<-*p+30Y<-*c6A<-*c120B<-*c0P<-&f1S
Death is now the phoenix' nest;
And the turtle's loyal breast
To eternity doth rest.

Leaving no posterity,
'Twas not their infirmity,
It was married chastity.
```

Figure 9-9. PCL Sequence for Vertical Rule in MultiMate. Notice there are no spaces between the first and second stanza.

Beauty, truth and rarity,
Grace in all simplicity,
Here enclosed, in cinders lie.

Death is now the phoenix' nest;
And the turtle's loyal breast
To eternity doth rest.

Leaving no posterity,
'Twas not their infirmity,
It was married chastity.

Figure 9-10. Printed Vertical Rule, used to annotate or highlight selected paragraphs.

This PCL sequence will draw a vertical rule just to the left of the margin. Put the sequence in the text where you want the vertical line to begin. For instance, if you want to annotate a changed paragraph, put the sequence on the line preceding the paragraph. Enter the PCL commands on one line so that MultiMate will repaginate correctly. The sequence should look like this on your screen:

E_C&f0SE_C*p-30XE_C*p+30YE_C*c6AE_C*c120BE_C*c0PE_C&f1S

Here's what this sequence does: first, f0S saves the current position of the cursor, because you will need to return it to its starting point for subsequent text to be printed correctly. Then, the p- command moves the cursor into the left margin one tenth of an inch, and the p+ command drops the cursor vertically one tenth of an inch. The purpose for dropping the cursor is to align the beginning of the rule more accurately with the text characters. Although that alignment takes a little extra effort, it's aesthetically pleasing. Try a vertical bar without the adjustment and you'll probably see the vertical line as misaligned and irritating.

The next two c commands set the width and depth (length) of the rectangle. To calculate the length, multiply the height of the text—in this case approximately .167 inches (6 lines per inch) times 3 lines equals .501 inches. Next, subtract the previous adjustment for the .1 inch white space at the top of the first line, and round out to .4 inches, or 120 dots.

The next command, c0P, draws the rectangle.

The last command in the sequence restores the cursor to its previously saved location in preparation for printing the text properly positioned.

All of this may seem like too much effort the first time through, but after you've practiced with a few lines, you'll come to enjoy the flexibility and value of your new skill and it will add to the appearance and readability of your documents.

HP LASERJET AND WORDSTAR

The WordStar feature for drawing vertical rules is the same one for drawing horizontal rules. But, just like horizontal rules, the vertical rules are built with characters, and the same limitations of weight, length, and placement apply. Thus, it would be difficult to place a rule in the margin of your document. In the next example, you'll learn how to draw vertical rules in the left margin of your document with PCL commands.

PCL does not have a line drawing command like Prescribe. The example below uses the rectangle drawing command instead to achieve the same goal. Here are the PCL commands needed to draw the rule:

Command	Explanation
E_C&f0S	Save the current cursor position
E_C*p-30X	move cursor position left .1 inch
E_C*p+30Y	move cursor position down .1 inch
E_C*c6A	Set rectangle width to .02 inches
	(6 / 300 dots per inch = .02 inches)
E_C*c120B	Set rectangle depth to 120 dots, or .4 inches
E_C*c0P	Draw the specified rectangle
E_C&f1S	Restore the cursor position saved earlier

```
Beauty, truth and rarity,
Grace in all simplicity,
Here enclosed, in cinders lie.
<-&f0S<-*p-30X<-*p+30Y<-*c6A<-*c120B<-*c0P<-&f1S
Death is now the phoenix' nest;
And the turtle's loyal breast
To eternity doth rest.

Leaving no posterity,
'Twas not their infirmity,
It was married chastity.
```

Figure 9-11. PCL Sequence for Vertical Rule in WordStar. Notice there are no spaces between the first and second stanza.

Beauty, truth and rarity,
Grace in all simplicity,
Here enclosed, in cinders lie.

Death is now the phoenix' nest;
And the turtle's loyal breast
To eternity doth rest.

Leaving no posterity,
'Twas not their infirmity,
It was married chastity.

Figure 9-12. Printed Vertical Rule, used to annotate or highlight selected paragraphs.

This PCL sequence will draw a vertical rule just to the left of the margin. Put the sequence in the text where you want the vertical line to begin. For instance, if you want to annotate a changed paragraph, put the sequence on the line preceding the paragraph. Enter the PCL commands on one line so that WordStar will repaginate correctly. The sequence should look like this on your screen:

E_C&f0SE_C*p-30XE_C*p+30YE_C*c6AE_C*c120BE_C*c0PE_C&f1S

Here's what this sequence does: first, f0S saves the current position of the cursor, because you will need to return it to its starting point for subsequent text to be printed correctly. Then, the p- command moves the cursor into the left margin one tenth of an inch, and the p+ command drops the cursor vertically one tenth of an inch. The purpose for dropping the cursor is to align the beginning of the rule more accurately with the text characters. Although that alignment takes a little extra effort, it's aesthetically pleasing. Try a vertical bar without the adjustment and you'll probably see the vertical line as misaligned and irritating.

The next two c commands set the width and depth (length) of the rectangle. To calculate the length, multiply the height of the text—in this case approximately .167 inches (6 lines per inch) times 3 lines equals .501 inches.

Next, subtract the previous adjustment for the .1 inch white space at the top of the first line, and round out to .4 inches, or 120 dots.

The next command, c0P, draws the rectangle.

The last command in the sequence restores the cursor to its previously saved location in preparation for printing the text properly positioned.

All of this may seem like too much effort the first time through, but after you've practiced with a few lines, you'll come to enjoy the flexibility and value of your new skill and it will add to the appearance and readability of your documents.

Chapter 10

Creating Boxes for Artwork

In many documents, a box that frames a graphic or that highlights a paragraph of text significantly improves the effectiveness of communication with your audience. Some word processing programs offer elementary box-drawing commands, but the resulting boxes are often rudimentary at best, and you usually have little or no control over the weight of box lines, or the precise placement around the items you want to emphasize.

By using the line and box drawing capabilities of laser printers, however, you can generate publication-quality boxes of all shapes and sizes, with just the right placement and line weights. The examples in this chapter shows how to draw boxes with you laser printer.

KYOCERA AND MICROSOFT WORD

Microsoft WORD has a built-in feature to draw boxes around text. However, the boxes are composed of vertical and horizontal bars, and the same limitations of line weight, size, and placement imposed on the lines limit WORD's box drawing function as well. Another limitation is that the WORD box command only works on a paragraph, so the only way to make an empty box for some other element, such as a space for a graphic callout, is to draw all four separate lines of the box. The effort to draw the lines separately usually outweighs the results. In addition, the corners may not meet properly—an error that never fails to catch the eye.

Creating a Box for a Graphic Callout

To create a simple box for an artist's illustration, type a Prescribe sequence in the text where the illustration is to occur. This example shows you how to center a 3-inch by 5-inch box in the text so you can add an image manually before publication.

To create the box, type these Prescribe commands:

Commands	Explanation
!R!	staRt Prescribe sequence
MRP .375,0;	Move Relative Position of cursor right .375 inches
SPD .05;	Set Pen Diameter to .05 inches
BOX 5,3,V;	draw a BOX 5" wide, 3" deep
EXIT;	EXIT the Prescribe sequence

```
                     Romeo and Juliet
 !R!
 MRP .375,0;
 SPD .05;
 BOX 5,3,V;
 EXIT;
 (Woodcut from ancient English manuscript)

          The scene:  Verona and Mantua

          CHARACTERS IN THE PLAY
```

Figure 10-1. Prescribe Sequence for drawing a simple box in WORD.

Before You Print

Here are the considerations to take into account when using this sequence. To position the cursor to draw the box in the center of the page, first calculate the distance to the center of the paper. On a standard 8.5-inch page, the distance is 4.25 inches. Then subtract 1/2 the width of the box and the width of the left margin currently in effect. Use this number as the X parameter in the MRP command to move the cursor horizontally. In this example, the X parameter is .375. To move the cursor vertically, substitute the number in inches for the y parameter, the 0 in the MRP command.

The weight of the line is set by the SPD command. The line weight on the Kyocera varies from .0033 inches (just a hairline) to .42 inches. The box command draws the box based on the horizontal and vertical values. In this example, those values are 5 and 3. The V parameter at the end of the box command sets the cursor at the left margin one line below the box in preparation for the text to resume.

The flexibility offered by these three simple commands allows you to control the shape, size, and location of the box on the page as well as the boldness of the border.

If you want more white space between the end of the text and the top of the box, you can either enter multiple carriage returns at the top of the sequence, or put a value in the Y parameter of the MRP command. To match the white space after the box, place the same number of carriage returns after the EXIT command.

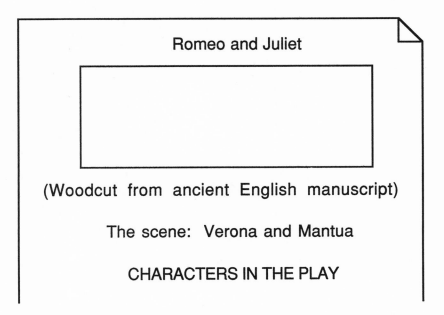

Figure 10-2. Printed box between paragraphs of text.

Multi-Page Considerations

In a multi-page document, adding a box with the Prescribe sequence may affect the pagination function of the word processing program. Essentially, the program doesn't "see" the box drawn by the Prescribe sequence and doesn't allow room for it in the pagination. Two methods can be used to correct the pagination: enter the commands on a single line, or save the sequence in a separate file.

The first method involves entering the Prescribe commands together on one line without separating them by carriage returns. If you use this technique, remember to separate each command with a semicolon. Next, change the last parameter of the BOX command to B instead of V. This will leave the cursor in the same location after drawing the box instead of moving it down one line. Next, place a .P. Code after the EXIT; like this:

.P. ,3

Make this short .P. code a separate paragraph. Then select it and either press ALT + E or choose Character from the Format menu and click on Hidden in the Format Character section. Making the .P. command hidden embeds it in the text, and WORD will skip the appropriate vertical space (in this case 3 inches) to allow for your box and will then continue pagination properly for the rest of the text in the multiple page document.

The second method of solving the pagination problem again uses WORD's .P. code feature, but this time includes a separate file in the text. The file has the Prescribe commands in it, and although it doesn't appear in the text, the printer will read the file and create the necessary space for the box. Because the file isn't in the text itself, the pagination will be correct.

To take advantage of this powerful feature, create a file that contains only the Prescribe commands for drawing the box. Be sure to use the V parameter in the BOX command so the cursor moves to the bottom of the box.

After typing the Prescribe sequence, store it in a file with an appropriate name such as 3X5BOX. When saving the file, select Unformatted on the Save dialog box because WORD cannot include a formatted file in the text. Next, you "include" the file by using the .P. code as follows:

.P. B:\3X5BOX.DOC, 3

Put the full file name between the .P. and the comma before the 3. Now, using the Character command from the Format menu, make this paragraph hidden text (as described earlier); before printing, choose Repaginate from the Document menu to paginate the pages of your document. When you print the file, WORD will include the external file, and send it to the printer, which will allow 3 inches of space during printing. The pagination will be correct.

One of the prime benefits of including separate files with the .P. code is that you can create a number of files for boxes of different sizes and line weights. Name them with self-explanatory terms, such as 3X5BOX, or Q1PROFIT and you'll be able to include them in any future document without re-keying the Prescribe commands each time.

Elaborating on the Simple Box

This next example shows how to add a second border to the box you created earlier. As you can see in the second figure below, the double-bordered box is a more elaborate frame for a graphic. To add the second border only takes three more Prescribe commands added to the earlier sequence. The new Prescribe commands are highlighted below:

Commands	Explanation
!R!	staRt Prescribe sequence
MRP .5,0;	Move Relative Position of right cursor .5 inches
SPD .02;	Set Pen Diameter to .02 inches
BOX 5,3,B;	draw a BOX 5" wide and 3" deep
MRP -.25,-.25;	Move Relative Position of cursor up and left .25 inches
SPD .05;	**Set Pen Diameter to .05 inches**
BOX 5.5,3.5,V;	**draw BOX 5.5" wide, 3.5" deep**
EXIT;	EXIT the Prescribe sequence

```
                    Romeo and Juliet
 !R!
MRP  .5,0;
SPD  .02;
BOX  5,3,B;
MRP  -.25,-.25;
SPD  .05;
BOX  5.5,3.5,V;
EXIT;
(Woodcut from ancient English manuscript)

        The scene:  Verona and Mantua

         CHARACTERS IN THE PLAY
```

Figure 10-3. Prescribe Sequence for drawing a double-bordered box in WORD.

The first BOX command is modified to leave the cursor in its original location, by replacing the V parameter with a B. Next, you reposition the cursor up and to the left 1/4 inch with the MRP command. Now set the pen diameter a bit heavier using SPD, and finally draw the second box around the first box with a 1/4-inch border. In the last BOX command, use the V parameter to place the cursor one line below the box in preparation for the text to follow.

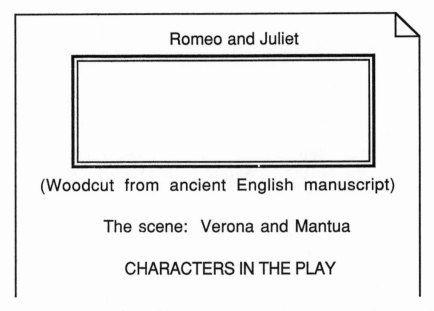

Figure 10-4. Printed box with double borders between paragraphs of text.

KYOCERA AND MULTIMATE

MultiMate has a built-in feature to draw boxes around text. However, the boxes are composed of vertical and horizontal bars, and the same limitations of line weight, size, and placement imposed on the lines limit MultiMate's box drawing function as well. Another limitation is that the MultiMate box command only works on a paragraph, so the only way to make an empty box for some other element, such as a space for a graphic callout, is to draw all four separate lines of the box. The effort to draw the lines separately usually outweighs the results. In addition, the corners may not meet properly—an error that never fails to catch the eye.

Creating a Box for a Graphic Callout

To create a simple box for an artist's illustration, type a Prescribe sequence in the text where the illustration is to occur. This example shows you how to center a 3-inch by 5-inch box in the text so you can add an image manually before publication.

To create the box, type these Prescribe commands:

Commands	Explanation
!R!	staRt Prescribe sequence
MRP .375,0;	Move Relative Position of cursor right .375 inches
SPD .05;	Set Pen Diameter to .05 inches
BOX 5,3,V;	draw BOX 5" wide, 3" deep
EXIT;	EXIT the Prescribe sequence

```
                    Romeo and Juliet
!R!
MRP  .375,0;
SPD  .05;
BOX  5,3,V;
EXIT;
(Woodcut from ancient English manuscript)

        The scene:  Verona and Mantua

           CHARACTERS IN THE PLAY
```

Figure 10-5. Prescribe Sequence for drawing a simple box in MultiMate.

Before You Print

Here are the considerations to take into account when using this sequence. To position the cursor to draw the box in the center of the page, first calculate the distance to the center of the paper. On a standard 8.5-inch page, the distance is 4.25 inches. Then subtract 1/2 the width of the box and the width of the left margin currently in effect. Use this number as the X parameter in the MRP command to move the cursor horizontally. In this example, the X parameter is .375. To move the cursor vertically, substitute the number in inches for the y parameter, the 0 in the MRP command.

The weight of the line is set by the SPD command. The line weight on the Kyocera varies from .0033 inches (just a hairline) to .42 inches. The box command draws the box based on the horizontal and vertical values. In this example, those values are 5 and 3. The V parameter at the end of the box command sets the cursor at the left margin one line below the box in preparation for the text to resume.

The flexibility offered by these three simple commands allows you to control the shape, size, and location of the box on the page as well as the boldness of the border.

If you want more white space between the end of the text and the top of the box, you can either enter multiple carriage returns at the top of the sequence, or put a value in the Y parameter of the MRP command. To match the white space after the box, place the same number of carriage returns after the EXIT command.

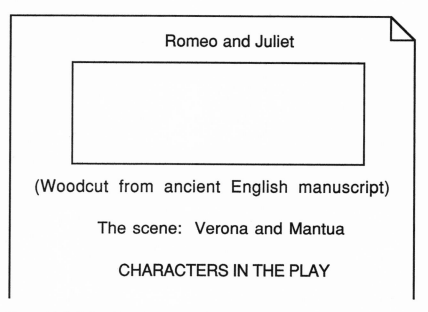

Figure 10-6. Printed box between paragraphs of text.

If your document is more than one page long, entering the Prescribe sequence as it's typed above can throw off the pagination. To overcome this problem, enter the Prescribe commands together on one line without carriage returns. Remember to separate each command with a semicolon. Next, change the last parameter of the BOX command to B instead of V. This will reposition the cursor correctly in the same location after drawing the box as it was before.

Elaborating on the Simple Box

This next example shows how to add a second border to the box you created earlier. As you can see in the second figure below, the double-bordered box is a more elaborate frame for a graphic. To add the second border only takes three more Prescribe commands added to the earlier sequence. The new Prescribe commands are highlighted below:

Commands	Explanation
!R!	staRt Prescribe sequence
MRP .5,0;	Move Relative Position of right cursor .5 inches
SPD .02;	Set Pen Diameter to .02 inches
BOX 5,3,**B**;	draw a BOX 5" wide and 3" deep
MRP -.25,-.25;	Move Relative Position of cursor up and left .25 inches
SPD .05;	**Set Pen Diameter to .05 inches**
BOX 5.5,3.5,V;	**draw BOX 5.5" wide, 3.5" deep**
EXIT;	EXIT the Prescribe sequence

```
                  Romeo and Juliet
 !R!
 MRP  .5,0;
 SPD  .02;
 BOX  5,3,B;
 MRP  -.25,-.25;
 SPD  .05;
 BOX  5.5,3.5,V;
 EXIT;
 (Woodcut from ancient English manuscript)

       The scene:  Verona and Mantua

        CHARACTERS IN THE PLAY
```

Figure 10-7. Prescribe Sequence for drawing a double-bordered box in MultiMate.

The first BOX command is modified to leave the cursor in its original location by replacing the V parameter with a B. Next, you reposition the cursor up and to the left 1/4-inch with the MRP command. Now set the pen diameter a bit heavier using SPD, and finally draw the second box around the first box with a 1/4-inch border. In the last BOX command, use the V parameter to place the cursor one line below the box in preparation for the text to follow.

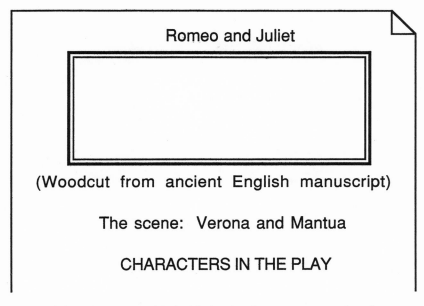

Figure 10-8. Printed box with double borders between paragraphs of text.

KYOCERA AND WORDSTAR

WordStar has a feature to draw boxes around text. However, the box-drawing feature is an extension of WordStar's line drawing feature such that the boxes are composed of vertical and horizontal bars. Thus, the same limitations of line weight, size, and placement that restrict line drawing apply to boxes as well.

Creating a Box for a Graphic Callout

To create a simple box for an artist's illustration, type a Prescribe sequence in the text where the illustration is to occur. This example shows you how to center a 3-inch by 5-inch box in the text so you can add an image manually before publication.

To create the box, type these Prescribe commands:

Commands	Explanation
!R!	staRt Prescribe sequence
MRP .375,0;	Move Relative Position of cursor right .375 inches
SPD .05;	Set Pen Diameter to .05 inches
BOX 5,3,V;	draw BOX 5" wide, 3" deep
EXIT;	EXIT the Prescribe sequence

```
                    Romeo and Juliet
!R!
MRP .375,0;
SPD .05;
BOX 5,3,V;
EXIT;
(Woodcut from ancient English manuscript)

       The scene:  Verona and Mantua

          CHARACTERS IN THE PLAY
```

Figure 10-9. Prescribe Sequence for drawing a single box in MultiMate.

Before You Print

Here are the considerations to take into account when using this sequence. To position the cursor to draw the box in the center of the page, first calculate the distance to the center of the paper. On a standard 8.5-inch page, the distance is 4.25 inches. Then subtract 1/2 the width of the box and the width of the left margin currently in effect. Use this number as the X parameter in the MRP command to move the cursor horizontally. In this example, the X parameter is .375. To move the cursor vertically, substitute the number in inches for the y parameter, the 0 in the MRP command.

The weight of the line is set by the SPD command. The line weight on the Kyocera varies from .0033 inches (just a hairline) to .42 inches. The box command draws the box based on the horizontal and vertical values. In this example, those values are 5 and 3. The V parameter at the end of the box command sets the cursor at the left margin one line below the box in preparation for the text to resume.

The flexibility offered by these three simple commands allow you to control the shape, size, and location of the box on the page as well as the boldness of the border.

If you want more white space between the end of the text and the top of the box, you can either enter multiple carriage returns at the top of the sequence, or put a value in the Y parameter of the MRP command. To match the white space after the box, place the same number of carriage returns after the EXIT command.

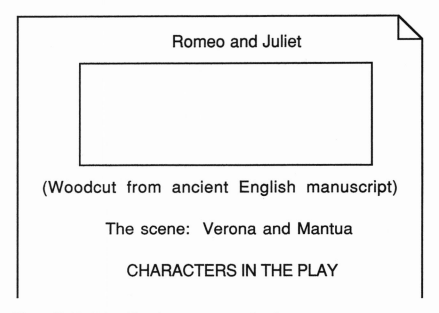

Figure 10-10. Printed box between paragraphs of text.

Multi-Page Considerations

In a multi-page document, adding a box with the Prescribe sequence may affect the pagination function of the word processing program. Essentially, the program doesn't "see" the box drawn by the Prescribe sequence and doesn't allow room for it in the pagination.

There are two basic methods to solve this problem. The first and simplest method is to enter the Prescribe commands together on one line, without carriage returns. If you use this method, remember to separate each command with a semicolon.

The second method for solving the pagination problem uses WordStar's .FI command to link a separate file to the text during printing.

To use the .FI command, first create a separate file that contains the Prescribe sequence for drawing the graphic to be included in your document. You can use carriage returns after each Prescribe command to improve readability and ease of editing. Because the commands are in a separate file, the carriage returns won't be counted by WordStar during pagination. Be sure to use the V parameter in the BOX command, to reposition the cursor the bottom of the graphic.

After typing the Prescribe sequence, store the document with an appropriate name, such as 3X5BOX. Next, link the file you've just saved by using the .FI command, like this:

.FI b:3X5BOX.pkg

When you print the file, WordStar will link this external file and send it to the printer with the rest of the document. The printer reads the file and leaves sufficient space for the graphic, but because the file is not "seen" as part of the text, the pagination is correct.

One of the prime benefits of linking separate files with the .FI command is that you can create a number of files for a variety of graphics. Name the files with self-explanatory terms, such as 3X5BOX, or Q1PROFIT and you'll be able to link them into any future document without re-keying the Prescribe commands each time.

Elaborating on the Simple Box

This next example shows how to add a second border to the box you created earlier. As you can see in the second figure below, the double-bordered box is a more elaborate frame for a graphic. To add the second border only takes three more Prescribe commands added to the earlier sequence. The new Prescribe commands are highlighted below:

Commands	Explanation
!R!	staRt Prescribe sequence
MRP .5,0;	Move Relative Position of right cursor .5 inches
SPD .02;	Set Pen Diameter to .02 inches
BOX 5,3,B;	draw a BOX 5" wide and 3" deep
MRP -.25,-.25;	Move Relative Position of cursor up and left .25 inches
SPD .05;	**Set Pen Diameter to .05 inches**
BOX 5.5,3.5,V;	**draw BOX 5.5" wide, 3.5" deep**
EXIT;	EXIT the Prescribe sequence

```
                    Romeo and Juliet
 !R!
 MRP  .5,0;
 SPD  .02;
 BOX  5,3,B;
 MRP  -.25,-.25;
 SPD  .05;
 BOX  5.5,3.5,V;
 EXIT;
 (Woodcut from ancient English manuscript)

          The scene:   Verona and Mantua

            CHARACTERS  IN  THE  PLAY
```

Figure 10-11. Prescribe Sequence for drawing a double-bordered box in WordStar.

The first BOX command is modified to leave the cursor in its original location by replacing the V parameter with a B. Next, you'll reposition the cursor up and to the left 1/4 inch with the MRP command. Now set the pen diameter a bit heavier using SPD, and finally draw the second box around the first box with a 1/4-inch border. In this last BOX command, use the V parameter to place the cursor one line below the box you've just drawn in preparation for the text to follow.

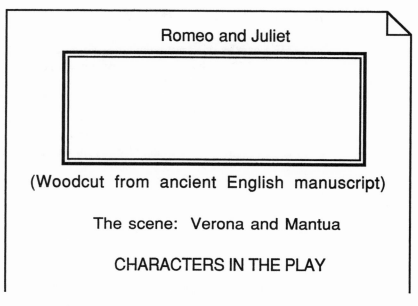

Figure 10-12. Printed box with double borders between paragraphs of text.

DRAWING BOXES WITH THE HP LASERJET

The HP LaserJet does not have a box command like the Kyocera. Instead, the LaserJet relies on character sequences or line drawing commands to create boxes. While boxes can be created using just the line drawing commands, it's a difficult task and usually not worth the effort. The main problem is getting the lines to meet at the corners of the box without overlaps or gaps. If faced with the task of creating a box with an HP LaserJet, you should use only the box commands available from your word processing program.

Chapter 11

Creating and Printing Logos, Signatures, and Other Graphic Images

With increasing regularity, graphic images are being included in documents created on personal computers and printed on laser printers. Often you may wonder, just how did they do that? In these next examples, that's just what you'll see—how *they* did it and, more importantly, how *you* can do it too.

WHAT IS "GRAPHIC" INFORMATION?

Graphic information is generally any information that is non-textual; that is, information not represented by characters that you type on the keyboard. It includes pictures, drawings, graphs, and many other kinds of non-textual information. One of the most popular forms of graphic information today is business charts and graphs that come from spreadsheet programs, such as Lotus 1-2-3.

Of course, there are more graphics than just numbers-into-charts. With today's sophisticated painting and drawing programs, you can create line drawings, schematics, and renditions without having to hire a commercial artist.

WHERE DO GRAPHIC IMAGES COME FROM?

You have several choices for getting graphic images into your PC. If you have artistic ability, you can draw the graphics directly on a PC with a painting program, such as PC Paintbrush®. If drawing isn't your strong point, you can scan images into the computer using a scanner, store the images as a file, and then, using a painting program, add your own touches to the images.

A scanner is a machine that, attached to your PC, translates images on paper into digital form. The machine has a slot where you insert the paper with the image on it. The image itself can be a drawing, handwritten notes, a signature, or anything else that you can draw. Using a process similar to a facsimile machine, the scanner scans over the page from top to bottom and converts the light and dark areas on the paper into a corresponding bit-mapped form that the computer can then process as digital information.

Images created with a scanner are very susceptible to even slight variations on the paper, and almost always contain extraneous spots on the screen rendition of the image. The image essentially looks "spotty." Thus, after creating a computer graphic with a scanner, the next step is to clean it up by erasing extra dark spots, as well as adding dark to areas that scanned as too light. Once the image is a true representation of the original drawing, you can then use a painting program to modify it even further. For example, you might want to erase a distracting background, or add your business logo to a scanned photograph.

Three of the most likely candidates for the democratic nomination of President of the United States are Jesse Jackson, Gary Hart, and Michael Dukakis who is favored by many to beat Jesse Jackson in the final tally.

Figure 11-1. Scanners offer you the ability to mix graphic images with your text documents to convey messages much more effectively.

Another method of getting graphic images into digital form is to use the graphing capabilities of various business programs. For example, Lotus 1-2-3 has the ability to change numeric information directly into charts and graphs. Using this kind of charting technique, you can create all kinds of graphs, and then electronically cut and paste them directly into some word processors or desktop publishing programs, such as Aldus PageMaker®.

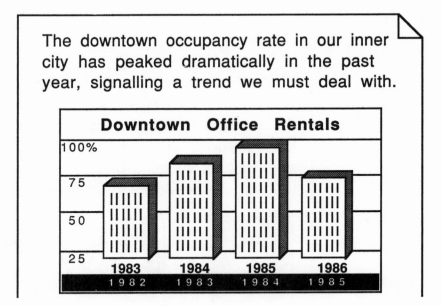

The downtown occupancy rate in our inner city has peaked dramatically in the past year, signalling a trend we must deal with.

Downtown Office Rentals

Figure 11-2. Business graphs can help tell a story much more effectively than just text alone.

The examples in this chapter illustrate the processes to create graphics, touch them up, and convert them to the proper types of files for printing on a laser printer.

PRINTING GRAPHICS WITH THE HP LASERJET

Although the HP LaserJet has the ability to print graphic images from painting programs or other programs with their own charting functions, the ability to print from a word processing program is difficult at best. In fact, the steps usually involve complex programming and an investment of too much time and effort. Consequently, if you are interested in printing graphics with an HP LaserJet, buy a program that is specifically written to produce and print graphics.

Because this book focuses on printing from word processing programs, the rest of this chapter is about printing graphics from a Kyocera laser printer.

PRINTING YOUR BUSINESS LOGO WITH THE KYOCERA PRINTER

This next example shows the process of printing graphic images, from start to finish, using the Kyocera laser printer. You can apply the principles in the example to your own specific word processing software.

Scanning a Business Logo

If you already have artwork of your business logo—for example, on your letterhead or business cards—scanning is the easiest method of getting its graphic into your PC. Follow the instructions with the scanning device you're using. Most have their own software to prepare the scanner to receive images. After running the scanner software, insert the paper with the image of the logo on it.

The scanner creates a file of the image. Save the file with an appropriate name, such as LOGO. Normally you can save the file in formats such as IMG, TIF, or PCX; the PCX file format is the bit-mapped format most widely used with personal computers. If your scanning software can't save the image in an acceptable format, or you need to do some conversion, scanners usually have conversion utilities to change the file from one format to another.

Using Painting to Create or Clean up Your Logo

Once the image is in a file, load your painting program, open the file with the image in it, and then use the program's commands and functions to clean up the image. When finished, save it again under a new name (so you'll always have the original scanned image available).

Preparing the Logo for Downloading

Now that you have a good quality logo in PCX format, you're ready to print it. The first step is to use the Font/Logo Master software from Kyocera to convert the PCX file into the LDF format. LDF format is for downloading either fonts or graphic images into the Kyocera for printing.

The Font/Logo Master software is also used to assign the image a font number, and divide the graphic image into bands, usually half an inch high and as wide. The first band of the image is stored as the letter A, the second band of the image is stored as the letter B, and so on until the each vertical band of the image is assigned a letter. In effect, by assigning each band of the graphic as a letter, you can print the graphic by printing each letter. This technique, you will see, makes the actual printing of the image is as simple as A, B, C.

Downloading the Logo to the Printer

When the logo is in LDF format ,it is ready to be downloaded to the printer. To accomplish this in DOS, at the prompt enter COPY LOGO.LDF PRN. This DOS command will transmit the file LOGO.LDF to the printer where it will be stored in RAM until the printer is turned off (or the file is explicitly deleted). The file can now be called for printing using a macro.

Creating the Logo Macro

The next step is to create a macro that will be downloaded to the printer, and used to actually print the logo.

Command	Explanation
!R!	staRt Prescribe sequence
RES;	RESet printer options to default
DELM LOGO;	DELete Macro named LOGO
MCRO LOGO;	create new MaCRO named LOGO
SCP;	Save Current Position
SCF;	Save Current Font
FONT 100;	Select FONT which is really the graphic image
TEXT'A';	print graphic image band in Letter A
MRP 0,.4333;	Move to Relative Position vertically one band
TEXT 'B';	print graphic image band in Letter B
MRP 0,.4333;	Move to Relative Position vertically one band
TEXT 'C';	print graphic image band in Letter C
MRP 0,.4333;	Move to Relative Position vertically one band
TEXT 'D';	print graphic image band in Letter D
RPF;	Return to Previous Font
RPP;	Return to Previous Position of cursor
ENDM;	END Macro
EXIT;	EXIT Prescribe sequence

Enter this series of Prescribe sequences into a new document, and save it as an ASCII file with the name LOGO.MAC. For more details on creating macro's, refer to the examples in Chapter 5.

Because it's not possible for you to type the actual logo used in this example, you won't be able to print a logo yet using this macro unless you already have file with a scanned image in it. Instead, carefully review the steps to follow, so when you have a scanned image, the macro will work for you.

Commands to note include the DELM command, which deletes any macro named LOGO, just in case you made a mistake on the first download. The SCP and SCF commands save the current cursor position and font respectively; they will be restored at the end of the macro in order to leave the word processing program in the same state that it was before the macro started execution.

The main section of the macro is next: the font number assigned to the graphic image in the laser printer is selected, then the TEXT commands print each succeeding vertical band of the graphic by printing each character in the alphabet. The MRP commands between the TEXT commands drop the cursor the appropriate vertical space after each band. This procedure is repeated until the entire graphic is printed on the page — as simple as A, B, C!

The text in the letterhead is printed as text in the macro. For clarity it is removed in the example, so that you can concentrate instead on the process of printing the graphic itself. Printing of the text is done in the normal way, and you can implement the text features described in Chapter 4.

Downloading the Logo Macro

To use the macro, you must first download it from the PC to the Kyocera printer. To accomplish this from DOS at the prompt, enter the command COPY LOGO.MAC PRN to copy the LOGO.MAC file to the printer. This command must be entered each time the printer is turned on.

To automate the process of downloading the macro, you can put the command in your AUTOEXEC.BAT file. Then, each time your PC is turned on, the logo macro will be automatically downloaded, and the printer will be ready to print graphics.

The next step in the process is to call the macro to have it print your logo.

Calling the Logo Macro

You can call the macro from either DOS or from a word processing program. When calling the macro in DOS, enter the DOS command COPY CON PRN to copy the contents of the console (screen) to the printer. If you are using a word processing program, skip the DOS command. Instead, enter the following Prescribe commands at the place where you want the graphic to appear:

Command	Explanation
!R!	staRt Prescribe sequence
CALL LOGO;	CALL macro LOGO
EXIT;	EXIT Prescribe sequence

```
!R!CALL LOGO;EXIT;
Dear Stefanie,

Thank you for joining our expedition to
Kathmandu next month.  I will be sending you
an itinerary within the week, so pack your duds!


                    Richard Bangs
                    Sobek Expeditions
```

Figure 11-3. Prescribe sequence at the top of a business letter, which will call the LOGO macro to print the Sobek logo on the letterhead.

If you have entered this Prescribe sequence in DOS, enter ^Z to close the file.

If you enter this sequence in your word processing program, place it where you want the graphic to appear and then choose the printing command. For example, when you include this macro at the top of your business letter, and choose the print command, the logo appears at the top of the page, and the body of the letter appears as you would expect.

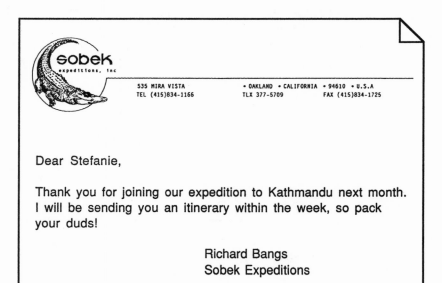

Figure 11-4. Printed page with Logo used as letterhead.

PRINTING YOUR SIGNATURE ON A BUSINESS LETTER

If you sign lots of business documents or letters, you might find it more convenient to have your PC and laser printer do the signing for you. The process involves creating your signature and storing it in a file as a bitmap, then using the same procedures described above for printing graphic images.

Scanning Your Signature

In order to get your signature into a PC file, you'll need access to a scanner. Prepare your signature for scanning by signing it with a medium-tipped black ink felt pen. That type of pen produces a solid signature that will scan well. sure to write on a clean, white sheet of paper to help eliminate some of the cleanup effort.

Scan the paper with your signature on it and then save the resulting file with an appropriate name, such as SIG. The next steps are the same as described earlier for a graphic image, except the macros are slightly different. Also, when entering the macro from DOS, remember to use the name of the signature file, such as COPY SIG.LDF PRN.

The macro for the signature file is:

Command	Explanation
!R!	staRt Prescribe sequence
RES;	RESet printer options to default
DELM SIG;	DELete Macro named SIG
MCRO SIG;	create new MaCRO named SIG
SCP;	Save Current Position
SCF;	Save Current Font
UNIT I;	set UNIT of measure to Inches
MRP%1,%2;	Move to Relative Position sent to macro as variables
FONT 200;	Select FONT which is really the graphic image
TEXT'A';	print graphic image band in Letter A
MRP 0,.35;	Move to Relative Position vertically one band
TEXT 'B';	print graphic image band in Letter B
MRP 0,.35;	Move to Relative Position vertically one band
TEXT 'C';	print graphic image band in Letter C
RPF;	Return to Previous Font
RPP;	Return to Previous Position of cursor
ENDM;	END Macro
EXIT;	EXIT Prescribe sequence

Enter this series of Prescribe sequences into a new document, and save it as an ASCII file with an appropriate name such as SIG.MAC.

When downloading the macro from the PC to the printer, remember to use the name you just assigned (SIG.MAC) so that the DOS command reads COPY SIG.MAC PRN.

The steps for calling the macro from DOS, are the same as before—enter the DOS command COPY CON PRN to copy the contents of the console (screen) to the printer.

If you are using a word processing program, skip the DOS command and enter the following Prescribe commands:

Command	Explanation
!R!	staRt Prescribe sequence
CALL SIG,	CALL macro SIG
4,1;	These two values are the X and Y coordinates in the MRP command, which will place the signature 4 inches over from the left margin, and 1 inch down from the current cursor position.
EXIT;	EXIT Prescribe sequence

```
Hi Larry,

Just a note to let you know that the logo and
signature graphics scanned in just fine.  I'm
printing them out now, and will mail them to
you in a few days.

                    Regards,

!R!CALL SIG,4,1;EXIT;
```

Figure 11-5. Prescribe sequence at the bottom of a business letter, which will call the SIG macro to print the signature graphic below the close of the letter.

As before, if you have entered this Prescribe sequence in DOS, enter ^Z to close the file. And if you're using a word processing program, enter this sequence at the end of your business letter, where you want your signature to appear. Choose the program's print command, and the signature will be printed in the letter.

Hi Larry,

Just a note to let you know that the logo and signature graphics scanned in just fine. I'm printing them out now, and will mail them to you in a few days.

Regards,

M Leube

Figure 11-6.

Chapter 12

Printing Barcodes with Your Laser Printer

From the checkout stands in supermarkets to movie rentals in video stores and inventory control systems in industry, barcodes have gained wide acceptance as machine-readable labels for an increasingly wide variety of items. The principal function of barcodes is to identify an object by a simple set of machine-readable bars that represent the characters and numbers of the alphabet. Being able to be read by a machine speeds the processing and control of items tagged with barcodes. Furthermore, the barcode reader reduces human errors and automates the tedious job of logging inventory, and auditing sales and receipts.

Traditionally, barcode labels have been created with special printers designed solely for that purpose. With laser printers, however, you can now print barcodes on adhesive labels. In fact, having the ability to create barcodes in a personal computer means that barcodes could be added to entries in a database. For example, if a database contains product listings, the barcode for each product could be part of the product's record.

In the examples in this chapter, you'll see how to print barcodes with your laser printer.

KYOCERA AND MICROSOFT WORD

One of the strongest features of the Prescribe language is its barcode printing ability. Barcodes printed on a Kyocera can range from .01 inch to 11 inches high, and from one dot to 200 dots wide. All 39 different barcode standards are available in the various shapes and sizes.

Because barcodes are read by special readers, the "scannability" or legibility of barcodes is an important factor dictating the quality requirements for the label. The size, width, and spacing of the bars are some of the graphic elements that affect the quality and that have to be controlled on the laser printer output. Scannability is also dependent on the quality of the paper.

The BARC command in the Prescribe language prints specified text in barcode form. Parameters of the BARC command allow you to control the size, width, and spaces of the bars. Experimenting with control parameters lets you find the best barcode for your particular application.

In the following example, the Prescribe sequence is for three columns of barcodes to be printed in two rows on a sheet of adhesive labels. The sequence describes printing sheets of labels with three across (known as 3-up). The label size is 2.5-inches wide and one-inch deep. To change the size of the labels, adjust the MAP commands in the sequence to fit the label sheets you are using.

To use this sequence with WORD, start the program and enter the sequence as if it were standard text. Select the WORD print command to send the sequence to the printer. When the Kyocera laser printer sees the sequence it will print the barcodes described by the BARC commands.

Command	Explanation
!R!	staRt Prescribe sequence
RES;	RESet printer options to default
MAP .6,.125;	Move to column 1 label 1
BARC 11,Y,'123011';	print the text string as a BARCode
MAP .6,1.125;	Move to column 1 label 2
BARC 11,Y,'123012';	
MAP 3.35,.125;	Move to column 2 label 1
BARC 11,Y,'123021';	
MAP 3.35,1.125;	Move to column 2 label 2
BARC 11,Y,'123022';	
MAP 6.1,.125;	Move to column 3 label 1
BARC 11,Y,'123031';	
MAP 6.1,1.125;	Move to column 3 label 2
BARC 11,Y,'123032';	
EXIT;	EXIT the Prescribe sequence

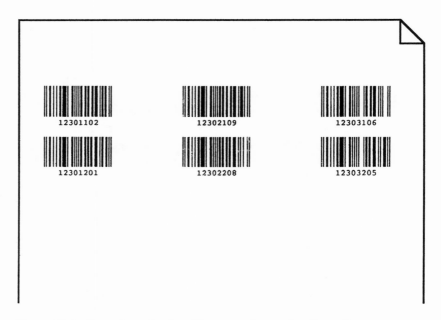

Figure 12-1. Barcodes printed on Kyocera printer using Prescribe sequence on 3-up adhesive labels.

The first number in the BARC command is a number from 0 to 38, designating one of the industry-standard barcode types listed in the Barcode Table in the *Kyocera Programmer's Reference Manual*.

The Y parameter in the BARC command indicates to print the text in the string that follows the Y as regular text under the barcode itself. The text is printed in the current font, which can be specified prior to the BARC command.

The actual text that gets coded into a bar code is entered at the third parameter in the BARC command. If you need more details about barcode printing to customize the example sequence to your particular situation, refer to the Kyocera technical reference manuals.

Before You Print

Some pages with labels on them will feed correctly through the Kyocera paper cassette; however, other pages are too thick and may jam the printer. If you suspect that your set of labels is too thick, you can set the printer to manual feed. To set it to manual feed, use the Prescribe command CASS 0 right after the RES command. Don't put it prior to the RES command. RES resets all options to their defaults, and the default for paper feed is "automatic."

Having the example entirely in Prescribe reduces the problems with pagination. Nevertheless, on long barcode printing sequences, you still may occasionally get a blank page of adhesive labels. This problem is difficult to avoid because the word processing program paginates based on the length of the Prescribe sequence, not on the number of labels being printed.

To reduce the number of blank pages, place Prescribe sequences together on one line separated only by semicolons, and set the printer page length to its maximum value. Be sure to set the top and bottom margins to zero to avoid having the top or bottom row of barcodes cut off by the printer. Not setting the margins to zero causes a problem because the printer cannot print outside of the area delineated by the margins.

One final step to help you avoid problems is to change the printer driver in your word processing program to PLAIN, TTY, or DRAFT. This change helps to alleviate conflicts between the word processing program, the laser printer, and the Prescribe sequence.

KYOCERA AND MULTIMATE

One of the strongest features of the Prescribe language is its barcode printing ability. Barcodes printed on a Kyocera can range from .01 inch to 11 inches high, and from one dot to 200 dots wide. All 39 different barcode standards are available in the various shapes and sizes.

Because barcodes are read by special readers, the "scannability" or legibility of barcodes is an important factor dictating the quality requirements for the label. The size, width, and spacing of the bars are some of the graphic elements that affect the quality and that have to be controlled on the laser printer output. Scannability is also dependent on the quality of the paper.

The BARC command in the Prescribe language prints specified text in barcode form. Parameters of the BARC command allow you to control the size, width, and spaces of the bars. Experimenting with control parameters lets you find the best barcode for your particular application.

In the following, the Prescribe sequence is for 3 columns of bar-codes to be printed in two rows on a sheet of adhesive labels. The sequence describes printing sheets of labels with three across (known as 3-up). The label size is 2.5-inches wide and one-inch deep. To change the size of the labels, adjust the MAP commands in the sequence to fit the label sheets you are using.

To use this sequence with MultiMate, start the program and enter the sequence as if it were standard text. Select the MultiMate print command to send the sequence to the printer. When the Kyocera laser printer sees the sequence it will print the barcodes described by the BARC commands.

Command	Explanation
!R!	staRt Prescribe sequence
RES;	RESet printer options to default
MAP .6,.125;	Move to column 1 label 1
BARC 11,Y,'123011';	print the text string as a BARCode
MAP .6,1.125;	Move to column 1 label 2
BARC 11,Y,'123012';	
MAP 3.35,.125;	Move to column 2 label 1
BARC 11,Y,'123021';	
MAP 3.35,1.125;	Move to column 2 label 2
BARC 11,Y,'123022';	
MAP 6.1,.125;	Move to column 3 label 1
BARC 11,Y,'123031';	
MAP 6.1,1.125;	Move to column 3 label 2
BARC 11,Y,'123032';	
EXIT;	EXIT the Prescribe sequence

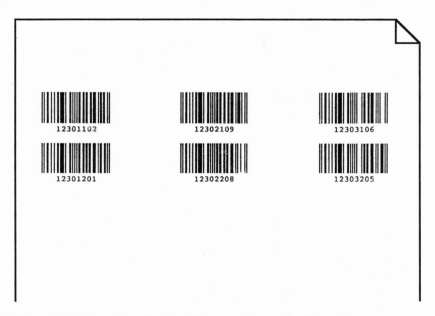

Figure 12-2. Barcodes printed on Kyocera printer using Prescribe sequence on 3-up adhesive labels.

The first number in the BARC command is a number from 0 to 38, designating one of the industry-standard barcode types listed in the Barcode Table in the *Kyocera Programmer's Reference Manual*.

The Y parameter in the BARC command indicates to print the text in the string that follows the Y as regular text under the barcode itself. The text is printed in the current font, which can be specified prior to the BARC command.

The actual text that gets coded into a bar code is entered at the third parameter in the BARC command. If you need more details about barcode printing to customize the example sequence to your particular situation, refer to the Kyocera technical reference manuals.

Before You Print

Some pages with labels on them will feed correctly through the Kyocera paper cassette; however, other pages are too thick and may jam the printer. If you suspect that your set of labels is too thick, you can set the printer to manual feed. To set it to manual feed, use the Prescribe command CASS 0 right after the RES command. Don't put it prior to the RES command. RES resets all options to their defaults, and the default for paper feed is "automatic."

Having the example entirely in Prescribe reduces the problems with pagination. Nevertheless, on long barcode printing sequences, you still may occasionally get a blank page of adhesive labels. This problem is difficult to avoid because the word processing program paginates based on the length of the Prescribe sequence, not on the number of labels being printed.

To reduce the number of blank pages, place Prescribe sequences together on one line separated only by semicolons, and set the printer page length to its maximum value. Be sure to set the top and bottom margins to zero to avoid having the top or bottom row of barcodes cut off by the printer. Not setting the margins to zero causes a problem because the printer cannot print outside of the area delineated by the margins.

One final step to help you avoid problems is to change the printer driver in your word processing program to PLAIN, TTY, or DRAFT. This change helps to alleviate conflicts between the word processing program, the laser printer, and the Prescribe sequence.

KYOCERA AND WORDSTAR

One of the strongest features of the Prescribe language is its barcode printing ability. Barcodes printed on a Kyocera can range from .01 inch to 11 inches high, and from one dot to 200 dots wide. All 39 different barcode standards are available in the various shapes and sizes.

Because barcodes are read by special readers, the "scannability" or legibility of barcodes is an important factor dictating the quality requirements for the label. The size, width, and spacing of the bars are some of the graphic elements that affect the quality and that have to be controlled on the laser printer output. Scannability is also dependent on the quality of the paper.

The BARC command in the Prescribe language prints specified text in barcode form. Parameters of the BARC command allow you to control the size, width, and spaces of the bars. Experimenting with control parameters lets you find the best barcode for your particular application.

In the following example, the Prescribe sequence is for three columns of barcodes to be printed in two rows on a sheet of adhesive labels. The sequence describes printing sheets of labels with three across (known as 3-up). The label size is 2.5-inches wide and one-nch deep. To change the size of the labels, adjust the MAP commands in the sequence to fit the label sheets you are using.

To use this sequence with WordStar, start the program and enter the sequence as if it were standard text. Select the WordStar print command to send the sequence to the printer. When the Kyocera laser printer sees the sequence it will print the barcodes described by the BARC commands.

Command	Explanation
!R!	staRt Prescribe sequence
RES;	RESet printer options to default
MAP .6,.125;	Move to column 1 label 1
BARC 11,Y,'123011';	print the text string as a BARCode
MAP .6,1.125;	Move to column 1 label 2
BARC 11,Y,'123012';	
MAP 3.35,.125;	Move to column 2 label 1
BARC 11,Y,'123021';	
MAP 3.35,1.125;	Move to column 2 label 2
BARC 11,Y,'123022';	
MAP 6.1,.125;	Move to column 3 label 1
BARC 11,Y,'123031';	
MAP 6.1,1.125;	Move to column 3 label 2
BARC 11,Y,'123032';	
EXIT;	EXIT the Prescribe sequence

Figure 12-3. Barcodes printed on Kyocera printer using Prescribe sequence on 3-up adhesive labels.

The first number in the BARC command is a number from 0 to 38, designating one of the industry-standard barcode types listed in the Barcode Table in the *Kyocera Programmer's Reference Manual*.

The Y parameter in the BARC command indicates to print the text in the string that follows the Y as regular text under the barcode itself. The text is printed in the current font, which can be specified prior to the BARC command.

The actual text that gets coded into a bar code is entered at the third parameter in the BARC command. If you need more details about barcode printing to customize the example sequence to your particular situation, refer to the Kyocera technical reference manuals.

Before You Print

Some pages with labels on them will feed correctly through the Kyocera paper cassette; however, other pages are too thick and may jam the printer. If you suspect that your set of labels is too thick, you can set the printer to manual feed. To set it to manual feed, use the Prescribe command CASS 0 right after the RES command. Don't put it prior to the RES command. RES resets all options to their defaults, and the default for paper feed is "automatic."

Having the example entirely in Prescribe reduces the problems with pagination. Nevertheless, on long barcode printing sequences, you still may occasionally get a blank page of adhesive labels. This problem is difficult to avoid because the word processing program paginates based on the length of the Prescribe sequence, not on the number of labels being printed.

To reduce the number of blank pages, place Prescribe sequences together on one line separated only by semicolons, and set the printer page length to its maximum value. Be sure to set the top and bottom margins to zero to avoid having the top or bottom row of barcodes cut off by the printer. Not setting the margins to zero causes a problem because the printer cannot print outside of the area delineated by the margins.

One final step to help you avoid problems is to change the printer driver in your word processing program to PLAIN, TTY, or DRAFT. This change helps to alleviate conflicts between the word processing program, the laser printer, and the Prescribe sequence.

HP LASERJET AND MICROSOFT WORD

Unlike the Kyocera printer, the HP LaserJet does not contain a built-in barcode printing capability. Instead, the HP LaserJet treats barcodes as fonts, which is somewhat limiting. Barcodes printed on an HP LaserJet use font cartridges X and W, or soft fonts that are downloaded to the printer.

Because barcodes are read by special readers, the "scannability" or legibility of barcodes is an important factor dictating the quality requirements for the label. The size, width, and spacing of the bars are some of the graphic elements that affect the quality and that have to be controlled on the laser printer output. Scannability is also dependent on the quality of the paper.

In the following example, you'll set up a three-column PCL sequence and print two rows of barcodes. The example is for printing the barcodes on a sheet of adhesive labels three across on a page, and each label is 2.5-inches wide and one-inch deep.

To use the sequence with WORD, open the program and enter the sequence as if it were standard text. Then select the WORD print command. When the LaserJet receives the file, it will read the sequence, interpret it as PCL, and print the barcodes.

Command	Explanation
E_CE	Reset printer options to default
E_C&l2H	Set paper cassette to manual input
E_C&l0L	Disable the perforation region
E_C(8Y	
E_C(s1p12v0s3b0T	
E_C&a280v540H(012345-GHIJAF(	
E_C&a540H(012345-GHIJAF(	
E_C&a540H(012345-GHIJAF(	
E_C(1OE_C(s0p10h12v0s0b0TE_C&a540H 01234567890	
E_C(8Y	
E_C(s1p12v0s3b0T	
E_C&a1000v540H(012345-GHIJAF(	
E_C&a540H(012345-GHIJAF(	
E_C&a540H(012345-GHIJAF(	
E_C(1OE_C(s0p10h12v0s0b0TE_C&a540H 01234567890	
E_C(8Y	
E_C(s1p12v0s3b0T	
E_C&a280v2540H(012345-GHIJAF(	
E_C&a2540H(012345-GHIJAF(	
E_C&a2540H(012345-GHIJAF(	
E_C(1OE_C(s0p10h12v0s0b0TE_C&a2540H 01234567890	
E_C(8Y	
E_C(s1p12v0s3b0T	
E_C&a1000v2540H(012345-GHIJAF(	
E_C&a2540H(012345-GHIJAF(	
E_C&a2540H(012345-GHIJAF(	
E_C(1OE_C(s0p10h12v0s0b0TE_C&a2540H 01234567890	
E_C(8Y	
E_C(s1p12v0s3b0T	
E_C&a280v4540H(012345-GHIJAF(	
E_C&a4540H(012345-GHIJAF(	
E_C&a4540H(012345-GHIJAF(	
E_C(1OE_C(s0p10h12v0s0b0TE_C&a4540H 01234567890	
E_C(8Y	
E_C(s1p12v0s3b0T	
E_C&a1000v4540H(012345-GHIJAF(	
E_C&a4540H(012345-GHIJAF(	
E_C&a4540H(012345-GHIJAF(	
E_C(1OE_C(s0p10h12v0s0b0TE_C&a4540H 01234567890	

Figure 12-4. Barcodes printed on HP LaserJet printer using PCL sequence on 3-up adhesive labels.

This is a complex-looking PCL sequence but, as you'll see, it contains a substantial amount of repetition. The first command sets the paper input to manual, and the second command disables the perforation region on the paper. Printing can then extend to the end of the page, which is often necessary when printing barcodes on adhesive labels.

After the first two commands, the remainder are broken into six groups. Each group prints one barcode label. By reviewing one group in detail, you'll see the difference in each, and will be able to modify the sequence, or create your own to print barcodes.

E_C(8Y	Selects the EAN-UPC barcode character set.
E_C(s1p12v0s3b0T	Sets all of the font options necessary to print barcodes.
E_C&a280v540H	Positions the cursor 280 dots down vertically, and 540 dots right horizontally. This is the only command that changes in each sequence by shifting each label down and over.
(012345-GHIJAF(	This series of numbers and characters must immediately follow the cursor positioning command. The left parenthesis is merely a bracketing sequence. The numbers and letters are

	the characters assigned to the barcode for the numbers 1 through 10. Obviously 1 through 5 work, but 6 is printed with G, 7 is printed with H, etc. The dash is a required delimiter, and the F at the end is a parity-setting character.
E$_C$&a540H	Positions the second line of the barcode directly under the first, by moving over again 540 dots. Note the lack of a vertical positioning command here; it is not necessary because the carriage return following the first string of numbers moves the cursor down one line correctly.
(012345-GHIJAF(	This is the identical sequence of numbers, printed on the second line.
E$_C$&a540H	Again, this is the horizontal positioning command for the third line of barcodes.
(012345-GHIJAF(	This is the third and final sequence of numbers, printed on the third line. These three print lines serve to make the barcode three times taller than the characters themselves, making it much easier for wands and other barcode readers to accurately read the barcode. Be sure to place each sequence of numbers directly after the horizontal positioning command, as shown in the example.
E$_C$(1O	This font selection command selects the OCR-B font from the same EAN-UPC barcode font, in preparation for printing the label under the barcode.
E$_C$(s0p10h12v0s0b0T	This the font selection command setting all of the font parameters.
E$_C$&a540H	This is the horizontal cursor positioning command for the readable label.
01234567890	Finally, this is the text for the readable label under the barcode. Remember, this string must directly follow the horizontal positioning command, as shown in the example.

By breaking down and inspecting each separate command, you can see the simplicity and repetition of the sequence. You can now modify this sequence for your own barcodes, or create a new sequence following the principles described above. For instance, to use the example with different-sized labels, adjust the column and label measurements in the appropriate commands. If you need further information about printing barcodes, refer to the Hewlett Packard LaserJet technical reference manuals.

Before You Print

Some pages with labels on them will feed correctly through the LaserJet paper cassette; however, other pages are too thick and may jam the printer. If you suspect that your set of labels is too thick, you can set the printer to manual feed. To set it to manual feed, use the PCL command E_C&l2H, right after the reset command. Be sure you don't put it prior to the reset command, because the command resets all options to their defaults, and the default for the paper feed is automatic.

On long barcode printing sequences, you may occasionally get a blank page of adhesive labels. This is a difficult problem to avoid because the word processing program thinks it is actually printing each line of the PCL sequence as text.

One final step to help you avoid other problems is to change the printer driver in your word processing program to PLAIN, TTY, or DRAFT. This change helps to alleviate conflicts between the word processing program, the laser printer, and the PCL sequence.

HP LASERJET AND MULTIMATE

Unlike the Kyocera printer, the HP LaserJet does not contain a built-in barcode printing capability. Instead, the HP LaserJet treats barcodes as fonts, which is somewhat limiting. Barcodes printed on an HP LaserJet use font cartridges X and W, or soft fonts that are downloaded to the printer.

Because barcodes are read by special readers, the "scannability" or legibility of barcodes is an important factor dictating the quality requirements for the label. The size, width, and spacing of the bars are some of the graphic elements that affect the quality and that have to be controlled on the laser printer output. Scannability is also dependent on the quality of the paper.

In the following example, you'll set up a three-column PCL sequence and print two rows of barcodes. The example is for printing the barcodes on a sheet of adhesive labels three across on a page, and each label is 2.5-inches wide and one-inch deep.

To use the sequence with MultiMate, open the program and enter the sequence as if it were standard text. Then select the MultiMate print command. When the LaserJet receives the file, it will read the sequence, interpret it as PCL, and print the barcodes.

Command	Explanation
E_CE	Reset printer options to default
E_C&l2H	Set paper cassette to manual input
E_C&l0L	Disable the perforation region
E_C(8Y	
E_C(s1p12v0s3b0T	
E_C&a280v540H(012345-GHIJAF(	
E_C&a540H(012345-GHIJAF(	
E_C&a540H(012345-GHIJAF(	
E_C(1OE_C(s0p10h12v0s0b0TE_C&a540H 01234567890	
E_C(8Y	
E_C(s1p12v0s3b0T	
E_C&a1000v540H(012345-GHIJAF(	
E_C&a540H(012345-GHIJAF(	
E_C&a540H(012345-GHIJAF(	
E_C(1OE_C(s0p10h12v0s0b0TE_C&a540H 01234567890	
E_C(8Y	
E_C(s1p12v0s3b0T	
E_C&a280v2540H(012345-GHIJAF(	
E_C&a2540H(012345-GHIJAF(	
E_C&a2540H(012345-GHIJAF(	
E_C(1OE_C(s0p10h12v0s0b0TE_C&a2540H 01234567890	
E_C(8Y	
E_C(s1p12v0s3b0T	
E_C&a1000v2540H(012345-GHIJAF(	
E_C&a2540H(012345-GHIJAF(	
E_C&a2540H(012345-GHIJAF(	
E_C(1OE_C(s0p10h12v0s0b0TE_C&a2540H 01234567890	
E_C(8Y	
E_C(s1p12v0s3b0T	
E_C&a280v4540H(012345-GHIJAF(	
E_C&a4540H(012345-GHIJAF(	
E_C&a4540H(012345-GHIJAF(	
E_C(1OE_C(s0p10h12v0s0b0TE_C&a4540H 01234567890	
E_C(8Y	
E_C(s1p12v0s3b0T	
E_C&a1000v4540H(012345-GHIJAF(	
E_C&a4540H(012345-GHIJAF(	
E_C&a4540H(012345-GHIJAF(	
E_C(1OE_C(s0p10h12v0s0b0TE_C&a4540H 01234567890	

Figure 12-5. Barcodes printed on HP LaserJet printer using PCL sequence on 3-up adhesive labels.

This is a complex-looking PCL sequence but, as you'll see, it contains a substantial amount of repetition. The first command sets the paper input to manual, and the second command disables the perforation region on the paper. Printing can then extend to the end of the page, which is often necessary when printing barcodes on adhesive labels.

After the first two commands, the remainder are broken into six groups. Each group prints one barcode label. By reviewing one group in detail, you'll see the difference in each, and will be able to modify the sequence, or create your own to print barcodes.

E_C(8Y	Selects the EAN-UPC barcode character set.
E_C(s1p12v0s3b0T	Sets all of the font options necessary to print barcodes.
E_C&a280v540H	Positions the cursor 280 dots down vertically, and 540 dots right horizontally. This is the only command that changes in each sequence by shifting each label down and over.
(012345-GHIJAF(	This series of numbers and characters must immediately follow the cursor positioning command. The left parenthesis is merely a bracketing sequence. The numbers and letters are

	the characters assigned to the barcode for the numbers 1 through 10. Obviously 1 through 5 work, but 6 is printed with G, 7 is printed with H, etc. The dash is a required delimiter, and the F at the end is a parity-setting character.
E_C&a540H	Positions the second line of the barcode directly under the first, by moving over again 540 dots. Note the lack of a vertical positioning command here; it is not necessary because the carriage return following the first string of numbers moves the cursor down one line correctly.
(012345-GHIJAF(	This is the identical sequence of numbers, printed on the second line.
E_C&a540H	Again, this is the horizontal positioning command for the third line of barcodes.
(012345-GHIJAF(	This is the third and final sequence of numbers, printed on the third line. These three print lines serve to make the barcode three times taller than the characters themselves, making it much easier for wands and other barcode readers to accurately read the barcode. Be sure to place each sequence of numbers directly after the horizontal positioning command, as shown in the example.
E_C(1O	This font selection command selects the OCR-B font from the same EAN-UPC barcode font, in preparation for printing the label under the barcode.
E_C(s0p10h12v0s0b0i	This the font selection command setting all of the font parameters.
E_C&a540H	This is the horizontal cursor positioning command for the readable label.
01234567890	Finally, this is the text for the readable label under the barcode. Remember, this string must directly follow the horizontal positioning command, as shown in the example.

By breaking down and inspecting each separate command, you can see the simplicity and repetition of the sequence. You can now modify this sequence for your own barcodes, or create a new sequence following the principles described above. For instance, to use the example with different-sized labels, adjust the column and label measurements in the appropriate commands. If you need further information about printing barcodes, refer to the Hewlett Packard LaserJet technical reference manuals.

Before You Print

Some pages with labels on them will feed correctly through the LaserJet paper cassette; however, other pages are too thick and may jam the printer. If you suspect that your set of labels is too thick, you can set the printer to manual feed. To set it to manual feed, use the PCL command E_C&l2H, right after the reset command. Be sure you don't put it prior to the reset command, because the command resets all options to their defaults, and the default for the paper feed is automatic.

On long barcode printing sequences, you may occasionally get a blank page of adhesive labels. This is a difficult problem to avoid because the word processing program thinks it is actually printing each line of the PCL sequence as text.

One final step to help you avoid other problems is to change the printer driver in your word processing program to PLAIN, TTY, or DRAFT. This change helps to alleviate conflicts between the word processing program, the laser printer, and the PCL sequence.

HP LASERJET AND WORDSTAR

Unlike the Kyocera printer, the HP LaserJet does not contain a built-in barcode printing capability. Instead, the HP LaserJet treats barcodes as fonts, which is somewhat limiting. Barcodes printed on an HP LaserJet use font cartridges X and W, or soft fonts that are downloaded to the printer.

Because barcodes are read by special readers, the "scannability" or legibility of barcodes is an important factor dictating the quality requirements for the label. The size, width, and spacing of the bars are some of the graphic elements that affect the quality and that have to be controlled on the laser printer output. Scannability is also dependent on the quality of the paper.

In the following example, you'll set up a three-column PCL sequence and print two rows of barcodes. The example is for printing the barcodes on a sheet of adhesive labels three across on a page, and each label is 2.5-inches wide and one-inch deep.

To use the sequence with WordStar, open the program and enter the sequence as if it were standard text. Then select the WordStar print command. When the LaserJet receives the file, it will read the sequence, interpret it as PCL, and print the barcodes.

Command	Explanation
E_CE	Reset printer options to default
E_C&l2H	Set paper cassette to manual input
E_C&l0L	Disable the perforation region

E_C(8Y
E_C(s1p12v0s3b0T
E_C&a280v540H(012345-GHIJAF(
E_C&a540H(012345-GHIJAF(
E_C&a540H(012345-GHIJAF(
E_C(1OE_C(s0p10h12v0s0b0TE_C&a540H 01234567890
E_C(8Y
E_C(s1p12v0s3b0T
E_C&a1000v540H(012345-GHIJAF(
E_C&a540H(012345-GHIJAF(
E_C&a540H(012345-GHIJAF(
E_C(1OE_C(s0p10h12v0s0b0TE_C&a540H 01234567890
E_C(8Y
E_C(s1p12v0s3b0T
E_C&a280v2540H(012345-GHIJAF(
E_C&a2540H(012345-GHIJAF(
E_C&a2540H(012345-GHIJAF(
E_C(1OE_C(s0p10h12v0s0b0TE_C&a2540H 01234567890
E_C(8Y
E_C(s1p12v0s3b0T
E_C&a1000v2540H(012345-GHIJAF(
E_C&a2540H(012345-GHIJAF(
E_C&a2540H(012345-GHIJAF(
E_C(1OE_C(s0p10h12v0s0b0TE_C&a2540H 01234567890
E_C(8Y
E_C(s1p12v0s3b0T
E_C&a280v4540H(012345-GHIJAF(
E_C&a4540H(012345-GHIJAF(
E_C&a4540H(012345-GHIJAF(
E_C(1OE_C(s0p10h12v0s0b0TE_C&a4540H 01234567890
E_C(8Y
E_C(s1p12v0s3b0T
E_C&a1000v4540H(012345-GHIJAF(
E_C&a4540H(012345-GHIJAF(
E_C&a4540H(012345-GHIJAF(
E_C(1OE_C(s0p10h12v0s0b0TE_C&a4540H 01234567890

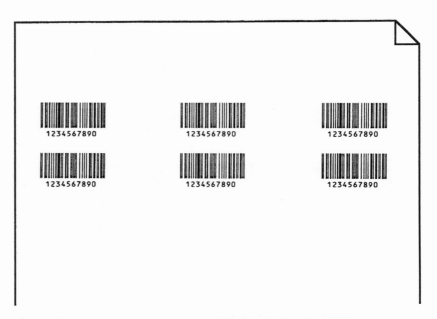

Figure 12-6. Barcodes printed on HP LaserJet printer using PCL sequence on 3-up adhesive labels.

This is a complex-looking PCL sequence but, as you'll see, it contains a substantial amount of repetition. The first command sets the paper input to manual, and the second command disables the perforation region on the paper. Printing can then extend to the end of the page, which is often necessary when printing barcodes on adhesive labels.

After the first two commands, the remainder are broken into six groups. Each group prints one barcode label. By reviewing one group in detail, you'll see the difference in each, and will be able to modify the sequence, or create your own to print barcodes.

E_C(8Y	Selects the EAN-UPC barcode character set.
E_C(s1p12v0s3b0T	Sets all of the font options necessary to print barcodes.
E_C&a280v540H	Positions the cursor 280 dots down vertically, and 540 dots right horizontally. This is the only command that changes in each sequence by shifting each label down and over.
(012345-GHIJAF(	This series of numbers and characters must immediately follow the cursor positioning command. The left parenthesis is merely a bracketing sequence. The numbers and letters are

E_C&a540H   the characters assigned to the barcode for the numbers 1 through 10. Obviously 1 through 5 work, but 6 is printed with G, 7 is printed with H, etc. The dash is a required delimiter, and the F at the end is a parity-setting character.

E$_C$&a540H — Positions the second line of the barcode directly under the first, by moving over again 540 dots. Note the lack of a vertical positioning command here; it is not necessary because the carriage return following the first string of numbers moves the cursor down one line correctly.

(012345-GHIJAF(— This is the identical sequence of numbers, printed on the second line.

E$_C$&a540H — Again, this is the horizontal positioning command for the third line of barcodes.

(012345-GHIJAF(— This is the third and final sequence of numbers, printed on the third line. These three print lines serve to make the barcode three times taller than the characters themselves, making it much easier for wands and other barcode readers to accurately read the barcode. Be sure to place each sequence of numbers directly after the horizontal positioning command, as shown in the example.

E$_C$(1O — This font selection command selects the OCR-B font from the same EAN-UPC barcode font, in preparation for printing the label under the barcode.

E$_C$(s0p10h12v0s0b0T — This the font selection command setting all of the font parameters.

E$_C$&a540H — This is the horizontal cursor positioning command for the readable label.

01234567890 — Finally, this is the text for the readable label under the barcode. Remember, this string must directly follow the horizontal positioning command, as shown in the example.

By breaking down and inspecting each separate command, you can see the simplicity and repetition of the sequence. You can now modify this sequence for your own barcodes, or create a new sequence following the principles described above. For instance, to use the example with different-sized labels, adjust the column and label measurements in the appropriate commands. If you need further information about printing barcodes, refer to the Hewlett Packard LaserJet technical reference manuals.

Before You Print

Some pages with labels on them will feed correctly through the LaserJet paper cassette; however, other pages are too thick and may jam the printer. If you suspect that your set of labels is too thick, you can set the printer to manual feed. To set it to manual feed, use the PCL command E_C&l2H, right after the reset command. Be sure you don't put it prior to the reset command, because the command resets all options to their defaults, and the default for the paper feed is automatic.

On long barcode printing sequences, you may occasionally get a blank page of adhesive labels. This is a difficult problem to avoid because the word processing program thinks it is actually printing each line of the PCL sequence as text.

One final step to help you avoid other problems is to change the printer driver in your word processing program to PLAIN, TTY, or DRAFT. This change helps to alleviate conflicts between the word processing program, the laser printer, and the PCL sequence.

Chapter 13

Printing Lotus 1-2-3 Spreadsheets

Working with spreadsheets is one of the most common applications on PCs today, second only to word processing. And of the spreadsheet programs on the market, Lotus 1-2-3™ is one of the most popular. In this chapter, you'll learn how to use your Kyocera laser printer to produce special printing effects on 1-2-3 spreadsheets.

Unlike word processor documents, most spreadsheets are printed horizontally on the page, which is known as the landscape mode (normal vertical pages are called the portrait mode). In addition, spreadsheets are often very data-intensive—that is, the information tends to be packed tightly on the page.

In this chapter's examples, you'll see how to select a variety of fonts, determine which font is best for your particular spreadsheet, and use macros to print special features from Lotus 1-2-3. By the way, most of these examples also work with the spreadsheet program named Symphony®.

BEFORE YOU BEGIN

For the examples in this chapter to work correctly, open Lotus 1-2-3 and configure it for the the HP2686A printer driver. This will set the program to operate with the HP LaserJet. If your laser printer is a Kyocera, use the Kyocera set-up software to make your printer emulate the HP LaserJet.

If you are printing with the HP LaserJet, the following examples do not apply because they all use Prescribe.

SELECTING DIFFERENT FONTS

Lotus 1-2-3 automatically defaults to Font 1, which is Courier 12 point Portrait. To change the font temporarily, choose the Printer Options Setup menu and place a Prescribe sequence there. This following sequence changes the font to Helvetica 8 point.

Command	Explanation
!R!	staRt Prescribe sequence
FONT 13;	Select Helvetica roman 8 point FONT *
EXIT;	EXIT Prescribe sequence

* See the Resident Fonts Table in the Programming Manual

Lotus prints information using a columnar format, so it is important not to use proportionally-spaced fonts. Those fonts will misalign the figures in the spreadsheet columns.

To make a specific font selection permanent, place its Prescribe sequence in the Worksheet Default menu under Printer Setup.

You can also place the font selection sequence in a spreadsheet's cells. Putting the sequence there will change the font for that cell, and then change back again to another font. You'll probably have to experiment with placement of font selection sequence, but it generally works well and produces an impressive output.

Any Prescribe command may be used in Lotus 1-2-3 to control its output. The Prescribe commands described in the section about macros may be particularly valuable because those commands can be placed into the setup string. However, the setup string only has room for 39 characters; therefore, the Prescribe sequence should be compressed as much as possible by eliminating all spaces that Prescribe does not require. As described in the section on macros, you can avoid the problem by putting a macro in the setup string.

GETTING THE MOST (PRINT) OUT OF LOTUS

One of the most bothersome problems of a spreadsheet is not being able to get all the information on one printed page. One answer to this problem is to use a compact font to print. The Kyocera printer has 18 different built-in fonts. The following table shows the fonts that will help you compact your spreadsheet information on the page. If you choose one of these fonts for your printing, set the left margin to zero.

Font No	Font Name	Orientation	Right Margin	No.Lines
1	Courier	Portrait	80	54
6	Prestige Elite	Portrait	100	70
15	Line Prtr 16.66	Portrait	150	78
16	Line Prtr 21.4	Portrait	200	94
25	Prestige Elite 16.66	Landscape	240	72
36	Line Prtr 21.4	Landscape	240	74

The lines-per-page is the maximum. Be sure to add lines for the header, footer and the seven lines Lotus adds automatically. The default printer settings are 66 lines per page, a left margin of 10, and a right margin of 74. You can change these temporarily in the Printer Options menu or permanently in the Global Default menu. The maximum page length in Lotus is 100, and the maximum right margin is 240.

THE MYSTERY OF THE CREEPING PAGE (AND HOW TO SOLVE IT)

Lotus doesn't send form feeds to the printer like most programs do; instead, it sends 7 blank lines between pages. Because today's sophisticated printers have their own printing programs, the 1-2-3 and the printer programs can sometimes conflict with each other when it comes to figuring out the number of lines per page. The result is known as page creep—each subsequent page will have fewer (or more) lines than the previous page and the spreadsheet seems to creep up or down on each page. While there is no sure-fire way to stop page creep in Lotus, using the settings and information in the following tables will, in most cases, fix the problem for the specified font.

You can modify the Prescribe setup strings depending on whether the page creep is up or down the pages. If the text is creeping down, then lessen the Lotus page length or increase the SLPP in the Prescribe setup string. Conversely, if text is creeping up, lengthen the Lotus page length or decrease the SLPP in the Prescribe setup string.

If adding or subtracting one line in both the Lotus page length and the SLPP command still doesn't doesn't fix the page creep, increase the SLPI by 1 to make the printer take up one less line per inch. Then retry setting the Page Length and the SLPP command.

The tables are set up assuming HP emulation, with the FonT MoDe (FTMD) set to 13, with the default of six lines per inch using the SLPI command. Page Length menu is reached with the Lotus command /ppop, and the setup string menu is reached by /ppos.

Courier 12 Point

Output	Page Length	Setup String	Text
Letter Portrait Normal	60	!R!FONT 1;EXIT;	80 cols 54 rows
Letter Portrait Compressed	82	!R!FONT1;SCPI12;SLPI8;SLPP82;EXIT;	96 cols 76 rows
Letter Landscape Normal	45	!R!FONT17;EXIT;	106 cols 39 rows
Letter Landscape Compressed	63	!R!FONT17;SLPP63;SLPI8.1;SCPI12;EXIT;	106 cols 39 rows
Legal Portrait Normal	80	!R!FONT1;SLPP80EXIT;	127 cols 57 rows
Legal Portrait Compressed	100	!R!FONT1;SLPP100;SLPI7.5;SCPI12;EXIT;	80 cols 74 rows
Legal Landscape Normal	45	!R!FONT17;EXIT;	96 cols 94 rows
Legal Landscape Compressed	63	!R!FONT17;SLPI8.1;SCPI12;SLPP63;EXIT;	163 cols 57 rows

Prestige Elite 10 Point

Output	Page Length /ppop	Setup String /ppos	Text
Letter Portrait Normal	60	!R!FONT6;EXIT;	96 cols 54 rows
Letter Portrait Compressed	100	!R!FONT6;SCPI13;SLPI10;SLPP100;EXIT;	104 cols 94 rows
Letter Landscape Normal	45	!R!FONT23;EXIT;	127 cols 39 rows
Letter Landscape Compressed	79	!R!FONT23;SLPP82;SLPI10.1;SCPI13;EXIT;	138 cols 73 rows
Legal Portrait Normal	78	!R!FONT6;EXIT;	96 cols 72 rows
Legal Portrait Compressed	100	!R!FONT6;SLPP100;SLPI7.5;SCPI13;EXIT;	104 cols 94 rows
Legal Landscape Normal	45	!R!FONT23;EXIT;	163 cols 39 rows
Legal Landscape Compressed	79	!R!FONT23;SLPI10.1;SCPI13;SLPP82;EXIT;	177 cols 73 rows

The Laser Printer Handbook

Letter Gothic 12 Point

Output	Page Length /ppop	Setup String /ppos	Text
Letter Portrait Normal	60	!R!FONT8;EXIT;	96 cols 54 rows
Letter Portrait Compressed	77	!R!FONT8;SLPP77;SLPI7.5;SCPI13;EXIT;	104 cols 71 rows
Letter Landscape Normal	45	!R!FONT26;EXIT;	127 cols 39 rows
Letter Landscape Compressed	63	!R!FONT26;SLPP63;SLPI8.1;SCPI13;EXIT;	138 cols 57 rows
Legal Portrait Normal	78	!R!FONT8;EXIT;	96 cols 72 rows
Legal Portrait Compressed	100	!R!FONT8;SCPI13;SLPI7.5;SLPP100;EXIT;	104 cols 94 rows
Legal Landscape Normal	45	!R!FONT26;EXIT;	163 cols 39 rows
Legal Landscape Compressed	63	!R!FONT26;SLPI8.1;SCPI13;SLPP63;EXIT;	177 cols 57 rows

Line Printer 9 Point

Output	Page Length /ppop	Setup String /ppos	Text
Letter Portrait Normal	60	!R!FONT15;EXIT;	134 cols 54 rows
Letter Portrait Compressed	93	!R!FONT15;SLPP95;SLPI9;EXIT;	134 cols 87 rows
Letter Landscape Normal	46	!R!FONT34;EXIT;	177 cols 39 rows
Letter Landscape Compressed	70	!R!FONT34;SLPP73;SLPI9;EXIT;	177 cols 64 rows
Legal Portrait Normal	78	!R!FONT15;EXIT;	134 cols 72 rows
Legal Portrait Compressed	100	!R!FONT15;SCPI19;SLPI7.5;SLPP100;EXIT;	152 cols 94 rows
Legal Landscape Normal	45	!R!FONT34;EXIT;	227 cols 39 rows
Legal Landscape Compressed	70	!R!FONT34;SLPI9;SCPI18;SLPP73;EXIT;	240 cols 64 rows

Line Printer 7 point

Output	Page Length /ppop	Setup String /ppos	Text
Letter Portrait Normal	60	!R!FONT16;EXIT;	172 cols 54 rows
Letter Portrait Compressed	100	!R!FONT16;SLPP100;SLPI10;MAP0,0;EXIT;	172 cols 93 rows
Letter Landscape Normal	45	!R!FONT36;EXIT;	224 cols 39 rows
Letter Landscape Compressed	95	!R!FONT36;SLPP96;SLPI12.1;SCPI23;EXIT;	240 cols 89 rows
Legal Portrait Normal	78	!R!FONT16;EXIT;	172 cols 72 rows
Legal Portrait Compressed	100	!R!FONT16;SLPI7.5;SLPP100;MAP0,0;EXIT;	172 cols 94 rows
Legal Landscape Normal	45	!R!FONT36;EXIT;	240 cols 39 rows
Legal Landscape Compressed	95	!R!FONT36;SLPI12.1;SLPP96;EXIT;	240 cols 89 rows

USING MACROS IN LOTUS 1-2-3

You've already seen how to set up the initial font in the setup string of the Lotus 1-2-3 Options menu. You can choose your initial page orientation, margins, and other options using Prescribe in the setup string as well.

Instead of trying to fit a sequence in the limited space of the setup string, you can put a macro calling sequence in the string. This next example illustrates the process of creating the macro and calling it from Lotus.

Creating a Lotus Macro

The macro can be created in DOS or in any word processing program. It is easier, by far, to create the macro in a word processing program than in DOS.

The Prescribe commands of the macro can either be listed on separate lines or on a single line. If you're entering the macro in DOS, first enter the DOS command COPY CON LOTUS.MAC. That command copies the screen's contents (which you will enter in a moment) to the file LOTUS.MAC. If you are using a word processing program, skip this DOS command. Here are the Prescribe commands to enter to create the macro:

Command	Explanation
!R!	staRt Prescribe sequence
RES;	RESet printer options to default
DELM LOTUS;	DELete Macro named LOTUS
MCRO LOTUS;	create new MaCRO named LOTUS
SPO L;	Set Page Orientation to Landscape
STM 0;	Set Top Margin to zero inches
FONT 23;	Select a landscape FONT of your choice*
SLPI 9.2;	Set Lines Per Inch to 9.2
SLPP 72;	Set Lines Per Page to 72
SCPI 13;	Set Characters Per Inch to 13
ENDM;	END the Macro definition
EXIT;	EXIT Prescribe sequence

* See the Resident Fonts Table in the Programming Manual

If you entered the macro in DOS, now enter ^Z to close the file. If you want to review the file in DOS, enter the DOS command TYPE LOTUS.MAC to list the file on the screen. If you entered the macro in a word processing program, save the file as an ASCII file with the name LOTUS.MAC (and be sure it has the .MAC suffix).

Now that you've created and saved the macro in its file, you can download it to the printer.

Downloading the Lotus Macro

Macros are small programs that reside in the printer itself. To use the macro you just created, you must first download the macro from the PC to the Kyocera printer. To accomplish this from DOS, enter the command COPY LOTUS.MAC PRN to copy the LOTUS.MAC file to the printer. This command must be entered each time the printer is turned on.

To automate the process of downloading the macro, put the command in your AUTOEXEC.BAT file. That way, each time your PC is turned on, your macro will be automatically downloaded and will be ready to use. Once the macro has been downloaded and safely resides in the printer's memory, you can call the macro at any time by placing the macro calling sequence in the setup string of Lotus.

Calling the Lotus Macro

Calling the macro makes the printer read its commands and execute the functions defined by those commands. Here are the Prescribe commands that call the macro. You enter this sequence in the Lotus setup string:

Command	Explanation
!R!	staRt Prescribe sequence
CALL LOTUS;	CALL macro LOTUS
EXIT;	EXIT Prescribe sequence

In other words, your setup string will include: !R!;CALLLOTUS;EXIT;

For this particular macro, the page length should be set to 72 and the right margin to 140. This will give you a spreadsheet consisting of 66 lines and 134 columns.

HINTS FOR PRINTING

Always Align the page before you print. Otherwise Lotus will place form feeds in the middle of a page when printing consecutive files.

When printing in Landscape orientation be sure to extend the right margin in the Print Options menu. Otherwise, printing may be cut off at the right. Extend the page length to the maximum of 100 when using very small fonts. You'll get the most on each page if you do.

You can print business graphs with the PrintGraph program in landscape mode by selecting the chart or graph, and printing in full size. However, the resolution of the graph is low. To convert Lotus graphs to 300 DPI, you can use an additional program to boost the resolution. One program that works well is the Laser Plotter program available from Insight Development.

Chapter 14

Expanding the Power of
Your Kyocera Printer

Kyocera laser printers have a unique feature that expands their power and capabilities. You can add an IC (Integrated Circuit) card to automate using custom fonts, creating graphics, or running macros. The IC card acts as a separate storage site for your custom applications that you can then access directly from the laser printer.

Probably the most visible benefit of an IC card is the automatic or transparent access to the custom fonts, special forms, and macros that you use every day. For example, instead of downloading a form from your PC each time you want print it, you can just put the form on an IC card once, and place the card in the printer. Then, each time you need to print the form you can just call the form macro from the IC card without using DOS commands to download the macro first.

Figure 14-1. Many varieties of forms can be created with Prescribe sequences and stored on the IC card for use in your business.

WHAT ARE IC CARDS?

IC cards are special memory cards used to store information. Conceptually, they work in a way similar to floppy disks: information can be stored on the card by writing to it, and information can be read from the card and printed by the laser. Some models of IC cards let you erase information from them as well.

Because the cards contain electronic circuits and silicon (special paper-thin glass) memory chips, you'll need to treat them appropriately. Never force the card into the slots, bend them, drop them, or expose them to heat, direct sunlight, or liquids. IC cards, like any devices that contains chips, are susceptible to static electricity. Never touch the gold contact points on the card, and always keep them stored in their original plastic jackets or other anti-static bag when not in use.

There are six different sizes of Kyocera IC cards, from 8K bytes up to 128K bytes. The designation K means 1,024 bytes, which is commonly rounded off and referred to as simply one thousand characters of information. To give you an idea of the amount of information you could store on the largest card, a normal page of information has approximately 2,000 characters. So, on an 8K card you could store about 4 pages of text, and on a 128K card you could store about 64 pages of text.

To help you estimate the amount of graphic information an IC card can hold, a two-inch square business logo that has been scanned into a bit-mapped image contains about 44K bytes. Add to that the macros you've written in this book to print the logo, and the total is about 45K bytes.

Many of the IC cards are called OTP cards, which stands for One-Time PROM. PROM stands for Programmable Read-Only Memory, and One Time means that you can only write to the card once, and only once. In other words, you get one chance to write information to the card and as soon as you stop, nothing else can be written on it. This feature assures that your information is safe from tampering because no one can modify the card after you've carefully put your information on it. However, because of this safety feature you should plan very carefully before writing your macros, fonts, or graphic images on the card. For example, if you only write a 5K macro on a 64K card, you'll waste 59K of space.

The other kind of IC card is the EEP card, which stands for Electrically-Erasable PROM. If you use EEP cards, you can add new information to your cards whenever you want and replace old items when they are out of date. The six different sizes and models of EEP cards will work on various Kyocera printers.

Kinds of Information You Can Put On an IC Card

You can put several different kinds of information on an IC card. The only limitation is that you want the information to be used directly by the printer.

One standard type of information for an IC card is a set of custom fonts. For instance, if you purchase a set of fonts or create your own custom set, you can store them on a card. Then, when printing a file, you can tell the printer to use the custom fonts.

Another typical form of information for the card is a business graphic that you will use often and that won't change. The most common examples are your business logo and personal signature. Having them on the card means that you can tell the printer to print from the card, instead of having to access other files.

You shouldn't store graphics on the IC card that are subject to change, unless you're using an EEP card. If you're using an OTP card, you can't change the graphic.

A third major category of information for the IC card is macros. For instance, you may want to customize the macros in this book, and then write them on the IC card. All of the macros in this book will fit on a single card.

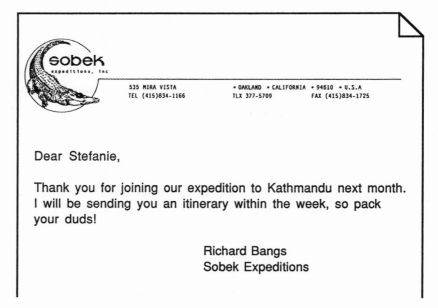

Figure 14-2. Logo's can be stored on IC cards and printed automatically when you print your business letters.

Perhaps one of the best uses of the Kyocera IC card, however, is to store your business forms on one or more cards. The forms can be complete with lines, instructions, fill-in-the-blank boxes, artwork, your business logo, large-type headlines, borders around the form, and even areas shaded with different levels of gray. You only have to create the form once (or scan it in), and then write it to the IC card. From then on, each time you want to print the form, calling it from the card is all the work that's required.

HOW THE LASER PRINTER USES IC CARDS

The IC cards work in a manner similar to your floppy disk in the PC. For example, when you want to use a macro that is stored on a floppy disk, you first download the macro to the laser printer. Or, if you've automated the process by placing the DOS copy command into the AUTOEXEC.BAT file, the macro gets sent to the printer each time you turn it on.

The same process is true of the IC card. When you turn on your laser printer, it checks each card slot to determine if any IC cards are inserted. If they are, the information is downloaded from the card into the laser printer's memory, just as it would be from a floppy disk or the AUTOEXEC.BAT file.

To use IC cards as the storage media for your information, you need the IC Card Reader/Writer Kit available from Kyocera. The kit consists of a reader/writer board and special software for creating custom IC cards. You install the board in your PC and use the software to write to the cards.

Installing your IC reader/writer card is a one-time process. The software, named the IC Card Utility program, lets you manage all of the information on the cards.

Writing Information to an IC Card

The following example explains the process of writing the envelope macro you created in Chapter 5 to an IC card. Having the macro on the card eliminates the task of downloading it each time you want to print an envelope. Not only is using the macro more convenient if it's on the card, putting it there also significantly reduces the time it takes to print each envelope.

If you saved that macro in a file, open the file and check that the macro is exactly the way you want it. If necessary, test the macro again to be sure it has all the right parameters and commands. Add any new features that you want. Here's the macro as it appeared in Chapter 5:

```
!R!
RES;
FONT 29;
SPO L;
CASS 0;
SPSZ 2;
STM 2;
SLM 4;
MAP 0,0;
EXIT;
Kyocera Unison, Inc.
3165 Adeline Street
Berkely, California 94703
!R!
RES;
EXIT;
```

Figure 14-3. Macros such as this envelope macro can be created and stored on the IC card to automate the process of printing special jobs such as envelopes.

Once you're certain the macro is correct, insert the IC card into the slot on the back of the reader/writer PC card (first.making sure that the PC is OFF) Then, power up your PC and run the IC Card Utility program, and follow the instructions for writing the macro to an IC card. This process of writing information to a PROM, which is done repetitively, is often called "burning" the PROM.

The process of burning a card can take from a couple of minutes to over an hour, depending on the model of your PC and the size of the card. As an example, burning a 64K byte card on an IBM PC or PC/XT takes about 40 minutes. During this time, the PC will write the macro literally thousands of times onto the card to permanently etch the information in the memory chips.

Once the information is burned onto the card, turn off the PC and remove the IC card. Now, making sure the laser printer is off, insert the IC card face up into one of the IC card slots on the printer. Turn on the printer, and it will automatically download the macro from the IC card into the printer's memory. Now you're ready to call the envelope macro from your word processing program without having to download it from your PC.

Reading Information from a Card

On occasion, you may want to read a font, a graphic image, or a macro from the card back into your PC. For example, you may want to update the information or change it, or even transfer it to another IC card. To read from the card to the PC, turn off the PC power and insert the IC card into the reader/writer slot.

Turn on the PC and run the IC Card Utility program. Follow the instructions for reading information from the IC card. The process to copy from the card to the PC only takes a few moments. Once the information is back in the PC, use the program you used to originally create the information to edit or change the information.

If the information is a macro, use the word processing program that you originally used to write the macro. If the information is a bit-mapped graphic image, use a painting program to edit the image.

A FINAL WORD ABOUT LASER PRINTERS

In this book you've seen a number of useful and innovative ways to put your laser printer to work. In the process, you've also seen a number of strategies for making seemingly complex things work smoothly.

More importantly, perhaps, is the introduction to the programming techniques that have shown how to make the laser printer achieve some of the types of printing that you've always known are possible. Using those techniques, you can now apply programming to other applications suitable for laser printing. Armed with your PC, laser printer, and appropriate technical literature, you should be able to tackle and conquer these new applications with confidence!

Index